Using Positive Psychology Every Day

We are all looking to flourish, to experience joy, feel engaged with the world, and experience meaningful lives. But the stresses and strains of our daily lives makes this a challenge. *Using Positive Psychology Every Day: Learning How to Flourish* is about (re)finding the art of living, enabling you to flourish.

Bringing together the best of positive psychology, this book introduces eight evidence-based resources of well-being and flourishing: positive emotions, the discovering and use of strengths, optimism, compassion, post-traumatic growth, positive relationships and spirituality. Each chapter has a concise, simple theoretical introduction and several evidence-based, easy-to-apply exercises.

This book is for anyone experiencing stress, distress or lower well-being, as well as coaches and therapists who can use the book for clients in the context of guided self-help.

Ernst Bohlmeijer is a professor in mental health promotion at the University of Twente. He has a special interest developing and evaluating interventions based on positive psychology, acceptance and commitment therapy and compassion-based approaches.

Monique Hulsbergen has been a psychotherapist for 18 years. She currently works as a trainer in compassion, mindfulness and well-being and is author of various self-help books.

Using Positive Psychology Every Day

Learning How to Flourish

Ernst Bohlmeijer and Monique Hulsbergen

Routledge
Taylor & Francis Group

LONDON AND NEW YORK

First published 2018
by Routledge
2 Park Square, Milton Park, Abingdon, Oxon OX14 4RN

and by Routledge
711 Third Avenue, New York, NY 10017

Routledge is an imprint of the Taylor & Francis Group, an informa business

British Library Cataloguing in Publication Data
A catalogue record for this book is available from the British Library

Library of Congress Cataloging in Publication Data
Names: Bohlmeijer, Ernst, 1965–author. |
Hulsbergen, Monique, author.
Title: Using positive psychology every day : learning how to
flourish / Ernst Bohlmeijer and Monique Hulsbergen.
Description: Abingdon, Oxon ; New York, NY : Routledge, 2018.
Identifiers: LCCN 2018001983| ISBN 9780815358343 (hardback :
alk. paper) | ISBN 9780815362234 (pbk. : alk. paper) |
ISBN 9781351112895 (epub) | ISBN 9781351112888 (mobipocket)
Subjects: LCSH: Positive psychology.
Classification: LCC BF204.6.B64 2018 | DDC 150.19/88—dc23LC
record available at https://lccn.loc.gov/2018001983

ISBN: 978-0-8153-5834-3 (hbk)
ISBN: 978-0-8153-6223-4 (pbk)
ISBN: 978-1-351-11291-8 (ebk)

Typeset in Stone Serif
by Florence Production Ltd, Stoodleigh, Devon

Contents

Introduction

This book is about the art of living.

The art of living has traditionally been an important topic within philosophy. There is, for example, the art of enjoying life, the art of developing one's own qualities, and the art of transcending oneself. The philosopher Michel Foucault spoke of the challenge of making one's own life into a work of art.

Also within psychology, the art of living has become a theme, especially in the current field of positive psychology. The psychological focus is on the same questions: How can I enjoy life and experience the joy of living? How can I develop myself and get the best out of myself? How can I give meaning to my life and experience connection to others and all of life?

The positive psychology we propose is in line with humanistic psychology. Our starting point is that we are all potentially unique, creative, spontaneous, talented beings and that every human being offers something valuable to the world. We carry that possibility within us. Even though you might not experience it right now, this also applies to you. We can neglect this possibility or lose sight of it. We can lose our individuality and originality. The art of living is the art of being who you are, of being able to once more create the space that you need to be who you are.

The objective of this book is, therefore, not to help you improve yourself. You are fine as you are. Perhaps this is more of a 'un-improve-yourself-book'. The art of living is more about letting go of certain patterns rather than about imposing certain requirements on yourself. It is more about creating space and about allowing yourself to be who you are, to be human, an experience which then becomes a source of joy, of self-development and connection. Carl Rogers (1961, p. 22) described it like this:

> The paradox that characterizes my experience is that the more I simply am willing myself to be, in the midst of all the complexity of life, and the more I am willing to understand and accept the reality in myself and in others, the more change occurs.

To be and develop oneself may sound easier than it is. For the art of living is not living life in a passive way. The art of living does not just come to us. It calls for the willingness to honestly look at yourself and take responsibility for your life. It calls for making choices based on self-knowledge and the knowledge of what is good for you. These choices inevitably bring along fear and uncertainty, which you need to be able to bear, like the fear of failure or the fear of losing the appreciation or love of people that are important to you.

As we have said, these challenges of the art of living have been around for a long time. The ancient Greeks and Romans have already contemplated these challenges. In some respects, the art of living seems to have become more difficult in our day and age. Society has become more complex, the demands put on us are high, and we seem to constantly be short of time. In other ways, life is easier nowadays, at least if you currently live in the Western world. There is no longer the daily struggle to survive. There is freedom of expression. You may believe what you want. Yet the challenges of the art of living are still as large as life itself. We are mortal with a limited number of years at our disposal, and we know we can die at any given moment in time. We also have to deal with adversity. And we are responsible for our lives, without having a detailed roadmap at our disposal.

How does it happen that we lose sight of our individuality, creativity and talents? How can our life stagnate? How can we lose the joy of being alive and the experience of meaning and connectedness? This loss can, for example, happen to children or adolescents who try to meet the requirements imposed by their parents or the school system. For fear of losing the love of people upon whom we depend, we give up our own thoughts and projects in order to adapt ourselves to the existing systems and profit from them. An adult can, for example, act exclusively with negative motivations. We can do things mainly or solely in view of minimizing our fear or uncertainty. Or we try to fill our needs whenever we feel that we lack something. Or we act in a certain way only in order to belong or to be seen or appreciated. We may do things mainly because we think they will make us happier in the future. Another cause of stagnation can occur when we are faced with a traumatic event or serious setback. It may be that we are unable to cope with it and then gradually grow embittered.

For mental health care, personal growth is a new, rediscovered focus. For a long time psychology has mostly aimed at reducing complaints and problems, and this focused allowed us to develop a great variety of interventions. Although this approach is an important improvement for many people, with the development of effective treatments for a variety of complaints, it also has its limitations. Perhaps our most essential insight is that well-being does not necessarily depend upon the absence of complaints and problems. It is possible to have complaints and still lead a satisfying and happy life, just as it is possible to not have complaints or problems and still experience life as unsatisfactory. The absence of complaints or problems does not necessarily lead to people developing themselves and finding meaning in their life.

Mental health is more than the absence of complaints. We can, therefore, speak of positive mental health. When someone has serious psychological complaints, embarking on a complaint-oriented treatment can help reduce the conditions that hinder life. But we also consider it crucial to focus as quickly as possible on the person's positive mental health. Positive mental health makes you more resilient and less vulnerable.

In this book, we describe the main themes of positive psychology. While reading this book, you can increase your positive mental health and well-being by shaping your life in a positive way that best suits your needs and your unique qualities. It is quite possible to actually achieve two goals at once – reduce your distress and accept what you cannot change. If you live in accordance with your inner values and you develop yourself, complaints can (continue to) decrease. At the same time, it is possible that a certain amount of complaints persist. And that reality calls for acceptance. Acceptance was the main subject of our previous book, *A beginner's guide to mindfulness: Live in the moment*. The present book can be read as a continuation of the first, allowing you to deepen the understandings you might have gained from our previous book.

The art of living consists, amongst other things, in your ability to find answers to the questions that life confronts you with. Everyone is faced with unpleasant experiences and adversity. In *A beginner's guide to mindfulness: Live in the moment* we described how struggling against unpleasant experiences only makes things worse. Literally, resistance only moves you 'from the frying pan into the fire'. On the other hand, the recognition and acceptance of these experiences gives you space to focus on what you consider important.

In recent years, research has examined the effects of our method of *A beginner's guide to mindfulness: Live in the moment*. We noticed that people using our book often named the same things (values) as being most important to them. Once they let go of their struggle against unpleasant experiences, most people want to focus their energy on what they value most. These values are, for example, to live life attentively, to enjoy life, to experience love and connectedness, to put personal qualities at the service of social goals, and to take better care of oneself. These are exactly the topics that positive psychology deals with, and we discuss each of these topics, helping you to apply the art of living to your life.

Objective and content

This book is meant for people who want to work actively at developing the best of themselves and others in order to experience joy and meaning in their daily lives and more of a connection to themselves and others. We summarize the art of living and this intention under the heading 'positive living'. In the following chapters, when we speak of 'living positively', we always mean living with the intention to appreciate what is present and to enjoy joyful experiences as well as developing yourself and contributing to the development of others and society. Living positively does not mean that there is no room for negative emotions, setbacks or suffering. On the contrary. In fact, it is not possible to live positively without being able to recognize and allow for negative emotions such as fear, sadness and suffering. This fact is, therefore, an essential theme in Chapters 5 and 6.

Each chapter presents a building block of the art of living – of living positively. Chapter 1 deals with pleasant emotions and experiences. The real art is to become more aware of positive experiences. Research shows that an increase in pleasant emotions sets in motion a virtuous spiral of creativity, increasing attention and personal growth. This calls for the appreciation of the positive things that are already in your life and for a routine of slowing down or even standing still in your life.

Chapters 2 and 3 are about discovering and using your strengths or qualities. We are used to being especially aware of our limitations and weaknesses and to work hard to improve them. When you start observing your strengths and using and developing them more, you will find more pleasure in learning. You will also discover that you are more positively motivated to develop yourself. This realization naturally brings more flow into your life. The essence of living positively is discovering what you enjoy and creating space for it.

Chapter 4 is about optimism and hope. A large role is played by your imagining what you would like to achieve.

Optimism and hope can be learned and will help you to achieve personal goals faster and more often.

The theme of Chapter 5 is self-compassion. Self-compassion is an essential part of the art of living. It is about recognizing and allowing your pain to exist and developing a friendly and supportive attitude towards yourself. The realization that suffering has been experienced by all throughout the centuries is a source of inner rest and resilience.

Chapter 6 is about coping with traumatic events and setbacks. Initially, difficult events entail much confusion and pain. It is important to make room for processing such experiences. Research shows that most people experience personal growth through these experiences. We discuss the factors that contribute to this growth.

Chapter 7 is all about relationships. Good relationships are very important to how we feel. We show how communication plays a major role in the development and deepening of positive relationships. We encourage you to think of how you react to the positive experiences of other people, of active listening, and of clearly communicating your own needs.

The theme in Chapter 8 is connectedness and giving. Research shows that selflessly serving others and acts of kindness are perhaps the biggest sources of joy and of personal well-being. Experience has also shown that self-realization by itself leads to the experience of belonging to a greater whole and of feeling part of the unity of all life. This experience then becomes a vital source of pleasant emotions and can strongly motivate you to discover the best of yourself and others.

Instructions for using this book

The suggestions in this book are meant to bring about a change in your attitude towards life. You are asked to reflect on how you want to live, on what gives you (long-lasting) happiness, and on the way in which you want to develop yourself. We believe it is worthwhile to take your time with this material, allowing the texts to affect you, as you complete the exercises with attention. You will find a large number of exercises and, naturally, you do not have to do them all. We suggest that you do invest time in the exercises that will help you to develop yourself and live positively. A good way to do that is to read a chapter and then do one or two exercises during the week. When you have worked through the book in this way, you can start again and then choose other exercises. You can also choose a theme that feels important to you in the moment and explore it at some depth. Hopefully, you will soon discover that you start taking pleasure in living positively, notice that it is doing you good, and develop a deeper sense of gratification.

If you are currently suffering from severe anxiety and depression, we recommend that you first seek help. The exercises in this book can become too burdensome, because you simply do not have the inner space for them. Also, it can be meaningful to seek help if you notice that the text and the exercises really make you feel off balance. It does not mean that this book is not for you. The fact is – while the exercises may sometimes seem 'light' – they can indeed be quite challenging.

Finally, your own way

Philosopher Martin Buber (2003, pp. 16–17) writes about everybody's unique journey of life:

> Every person born into this world represents something new, something that never existed before, something original and unique . . . Every single man is a new thing in the world, and is called upon to fulfil his particularity in the world . . . Every man's foremost task is the actualization of his unique, unprecedented and never reoccurring potentialities, and not the repetition of something that another, and it could even be the greatest, has already achieved . . . Rabbi

> Zusya said, a short while before his death: "In the world to come, I shall not be asked: 'Why were you not Moses?' I shall be asked: "Why were you not Zusya?'"

This book is about discovering a turning point in your life, from being negatively motivated towards living a life full of positive motivation. That is a leap. When we live from a negatively motivated point of view, we are focused on reducing our anxiety and decreasing any weaknesses we might experience. We try to guard against possible threats and to stay on the safe side of life, which can prompt us to adapt and conform. This approach is certainly not always wrong and can sometimes even be necessary. But in the long run, it may become a burden. Living with a positively motivated perspective means that we are focused on personal growth. Life becomes a personal journey of adventure, which includes uncertainty. But when you choose this path, you will find it to be incredibly rewarding. You will discover a sense of satisfaction that will make you long for more, and before you realize it, you no longer want anything else.

You have but one certainty – you are alive. You were born and you know that you will die. This is your life. It is up to you to determine what you want to do with it.

References

Bohlmeijer, E.T. and Hulsbergen, M.L. (2013). *A beginner's guide to mindfulness: Live in the moment.* London: McGraw-Hill.

Buber, M. (2003). *De weg van de mens. (The way of man).* Utrecht/Antwerpen: Kosmos – Z&K Uitgevers.

Rogers, C.R. (1961). *On becoming a person: A therapist's view of psychotherapy.* London: Constable.

Chapter 1

High time for joy

Introduction

The field of psychology has been dedicated mostly to unpleasant emotions, such as fear, grief, loneliness, sadness, shame, and aggression. Many theories have been developed regarding the underlying causes of unpleasant emotions and the things needed to mitigate their effects. This is understandable, because the long-held guiding principle was that unpleasant experiences hinder our happiness. Therapy can help take the edges off of our emotions. Nevertheless, unpleasant emotions are never fully erased and research has shown that we can become stranded in our endless quest to attempt to control these emotions (Hayes et al., 2004). Little attention was paid to pleasant emotions in psychology. In your own life, you too may hardly be aware of the moments when you experience pleasant emotions, such as happiness or love. You take them for granted, even though recent studies, which we will discuss below, demonstrate that this is not justified. In this chapter, we discuss how experiencing pleasant emotions is a major key to positive living. First we will explain why this is the case. Then, we will provide you with exercises that can help you experience more pleasant emotions. We would like to invite you to experience what happens once you focus your attention on pleasant emotions.

The importance of pleasant emotions

Tomorrow, take the time to observe your surroundings. What do you see in the faces on people you see in the street? Do they seem happy, good-natured, full of joy, extroverted; or do they seem surly, unhappy, burdened, tense, harried, introverted? How about at work? What is the mood like? How do people respond to each other?

You may note that people's emotions and interactions sometimes appear to default to negative instead of positive. People seem to pay more attention to what is going wrong, to what is missing. There are, of course, countless exceptions – but generally speaking, our society seems to have in store more unpleasant experiences than pleasant ones. The news you read in newspapers or see on TV tends to emphasize negative events. Complaints and gossip are always lurking around the corner. It is as though our communications are more easily influenced by unpleasant emotions. It also seems to be part of our lifestyle – so much to do, so little time to do it, rushing off our feet, barely being able to truly relax, always working hard in pursuit of success, all the while trying to show the outside world what wonderful people we are. And all this effort comes at a price. Fatigue. Depression. Addiction. Fear. In short, many of us seem caught up in a life of effort and ambition. This makes it hard for us to hold on to our awareness, and to enjoy the pleasant aspects of life; it makes it hard to be inspired. Our capacity for long-lasting satisfaction and happiness seems to be missing. The emphasis is on quantity, instead of quality, of life.

This book distinguishes between pleasant and unpleasant emotions. The field of psychology often uses the terms 'positive' and 'negative', which may lead you to think that it is the emotion itself that is negative. But despite the connotations of these terms, no emotion is inherently negative since they all fulfil an important role in our survival. Anger, grief, and sadness are generally perceived to be unpleasant, and can have destructive consequences if they are not recognized or expressed in a constructive manner. This chapter focuses on enhancing pleasant emotions, without covering up or suppressing unpleasant ones. Chapters 5 (on compassion) and 6 (on post-traumatic growth) discuss ways of dealing with unpleasant emotions.

Ten pleasant emotions

Being happy in your daily life and work is no easy feat. An important key to inspired living, to experiencing joy, is reinforcing the way you experience pleasant emotions every day. Barbara Fredrickson is an American professor who has conducted a lot of research into pleasant emotions. In this chapter, we are letting her work inspire us.

In her book *Positivity*, Fredrickson (2009) distinguishes between ten pleasant emotions:

- Joy
  The feeling of happiness and delight you experience when something good happens to you, or when you are doing something you enjoy. This emotion makes you feel alive and unburdened.
- Gratitude
  The feeling you experience when you receive something, especially if something performs an unexpected favour or if a situation turns to your advantage. Feeling privileged. Do not confuse this with the feeling that you owe someone a favour in return.
- Calm
  Those moments where you are completely at peace, harmonious. Frequently achieved following some amount of effort.
- Interest
  Something new has caught your attention. You feel the urge to find out more, to learn, to master.
- Hope
  A potential boon during times of hardship. You feel and know from experience that things will get better.
- Pride
  A feeling that is often the result of your expectation that others will appreciate something you have done or

achieved. For this reason, it is also referred to as a self-aware emotion. Ranks slightly stronger than satisfaction.

- Cheer
  Strongly linked to humour and conviviality.
- Inspiration
  You feel touched by someone or something, and you feel the urge to explore, to turn over a new leaf. This is often the result of seeing someone do something remarkable.
- Awe
  What you experience when, for example, you are impressed by a natural phenomenon, or by someone's kindness or wisdom.
- Love
  This encompasses and reinforces the other pleasant emotions. Often within the context of an intimate relationship or friendship. A many-faceted feeling to be certain.

Particular characteristics of pleasant emotions

The following are some notable points to consider with respect to the overview of pleasant emotions:

- Most pleasant emotions are experienced mainly when we feel safe and calm, when we feel we have all the time in the world, when we are tranquilly present in the here-and-now. This applies particularly to awe and calmness. The exception is hope: Hope is an emotion linked to times of adversity, to times of hardship. Hope is the confidence that things are going to change for the better in the foreseeable future. Restlessness, agitation, hurriedness all create a context in which pleasant emotions are felt and experienced less quickly.
- Some emotions are strongly linked to personal challenges and growth. For example, we feel proud when we succeed in completing a difficult challenge. Inspiration and interest drive us to explore the unknown, and to set new goals for ourselves.

- Other emotions let us rise above ourselves, such as gratitude, awe, love, and inspiration. They connect us to other
people; they are accompanied by a feeling that we are
part of a greater whole, and motivate us to commit to a
common goal.

The importance of pleasant emotions

Why are pleasant emotions so important? Based on scien-
tific experiments into the effects of pleasant emotions,
Frederickson formulated a theory she called *broaden and build*.
Here is a brief explanation:

Broaden

Before you read on, here is a little experiment for you.[1]

- Grab a pen and paper.
- Take a minute or two to have a good look at the top of
your hand. What do you see? What is the colour of your
skin? What lines or veins can you make out? What do
you notice around your knuckles?
- Pick up your pen. Imagine you have a free hour to spend.
How would you spend it? Write down the possibilities
you think of.
- Put down your pen. Close your eyes. Think of a moment
in your life when you were very happy. Immerse yourself
in this moment. Try to relive it. What happened? How
did you feel?
- Pick up your pen again. Again, image you have a free
hour to spend. How would you spend it? Make a list.
- Have a look at your two lists. Which list is longer? For
most people, this will be the second one: That is the
power of pleasant emotions. The initial situation (looking
at your hand) was a neutral experience. For the second
situation, you first improved your mood.

Fredrickson discovered that pleasant emotions broaden our attention span, while unpleasant emotions narrow it. If you feel uncomfortable, your thought processes become rigid, and you turn your attention to whatever it is that is making you sad or angry. You become trapped in repetitive patterns of action and thought. You will be more prone to errors because you fail to notice possibilities or pitfalls. You close yourself off from other people, and you become defensive. When you feel comfortable, you can take a broader view and open up. You regain your grip on the situation, improve your flexibility, and find new possibilities. As a result, you become more sensitive to your surroundings, and improve your understanding of what is actually happening. Your broad view helps you think of more and better solutions, even when dealing with misfortune or adversity. Your thought processes become more creative, you feel more connected to other people, and you become more supportive, generous, and forgiving.

There have been many experiments which have demonstrated the existence of the 'broaden-effect'. One experiment faced the test subjects with various figures. It was possible to view these figures as individual elements, but they could also have been viewed as being part of a greater whole. The test subjects who took part in the experiment while in a pleasant mood more frequently saw the greater whole than test subjects in a neutral or unpleasant mood. Pleasant emotions appear to refocus our attention on a situation as a whole.

Another experiment showed test subjects a series of images depicting increasingly overlapping circles. Here are three examples:

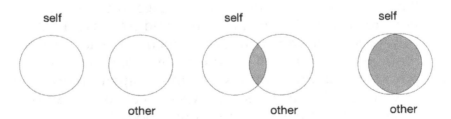

Figure 1.1 Self other

These images are used in studies to predict the level of connectedness within relationships. The greater the overlap between circles, the greater the level of connectedness. The greater the level of connectedness experienced by partners, the greater the chance of a successful relationship. The idea behind this is that love makes you view your partner's characteristics as your own. This is known as 'self-expansion', which we will cover in a little more detail in Chapter 7. Test subjects who had been put in a positive mood tended to pick the figures showing greater overlap.

Another experiment had test subjects take part in a word game; they had to provide a word which linked three other given words. This experiment demonstrated verbal creativity. For example: The three words are 'manners', 'round', and 'tennis'; the answer: 'table'. Test subjects who had been put in a pleasant mood were more successful at finding the right answer than test subjects who had not been put in a pleasant mood.

Research by Bryant and Veroff (2007) divided participants into three groups. These groups were told to go for a walk. The first group did not receive any additional assignment; the second group was told to focus on negative things during their walk, such as litter; and the third group was instructed to have fun, and focus on positive things, such as flowers or birdsong. When the groups returned from their walks, the people in the third group turned out to be feeling happier than participants in the other two groups.

These are just a few examples of studies indicating that feeling pleasant emotions leads to broader perceptions, increased connectedness, and improved creativity.

Build

In addition to broadening, Fredrickson describes a second effect of experiencing pleasant emotions: the building up of mental, psychological, physical, and social resources. Becoming more creative and open triggers a positive chain reaction. This chain reaction includes the following aspects:

15

- Making good choices and coming up with effective solutions;
- Developing confidence in your own abilities;
- Becoming inspired and, as a result, formulating meaningful goals;
- Being able to enjoy a fun activity as a result of increased awareness of your actions;
- Increasing your desire for healthy living and exercise;
- Becoming milder towards yourself and improving your self-acceptance;
- Reinforcing friendships and relationships as a result of your becoming more attentive to the needs of others;
- Generating a reciprocal effect as other people begin to appreciate your personal improvements, leading to a positive change in their own mood, feeding back your own kindness and attentiveness into your system; and
- Improving your strength and resilience.

Experiencing pleasant emotions – exercises

The first two exercises are mainly intended to increase your insight into when and how often you experience pleasant emotions. These are followed by a number of exercises which are aimed directly at enhancing pleasant emotions.

Exercise 1: Diary of pleasant emotions

This week, make a note of when you experienced pleasant emotions. For example, every evening take a moment to consider moments of joy, pride, hopefulness, gratitude, etc. Describe what was happening. Who were you with? What were you doing? How long did it take? You can also write down what, if anything, made the emotion go away. It is particularly interesting to note whether specific thoughts broke the spell.

Table 1.1 Diary of pleasant experiences and emotions

Day of the week	What was happening? Who were you with and what were you doing? Which of the positive emotions did you experience?	What made it stop? Was there a particular thought you had that played a part in this?	How good were you feeling at the positive moment? Rate it on a scale from 0 (unpleasant) to 10 (pleasant).
Monday			
Tuesday			
Wednesday			
Thursday			
Friday			
Saturday			
Sunday			

What do you notice following the end of this week? Are there particular thoughts that seem to recur?

Exercise 2: How many pleasant emotions do you experience?

The following is a brief questionnaire that will help you determine to what extent you experience pleasant emotions:

Table 1.2 Ten questions on emotions

	These questions are concerned with your feelings over the past 24 hours. Rate, on a scale of 0 to 4, to what extent you experienced these emotions: 0 = not at all, 1 = slightly, 2 = reasonably strongly, 3 = rather strongly, 4 = very strongly	Rating
1	To what extent did you have fun or feel enjoyment?	
2	To what extent did you feel love, closeness or trust?	
3	To what extent did you feel calm, satisfied or at peace?	
4	To what extent did you feel admiration, awe or surprise?	
5	To what extent did you feel happiness or joy?	
6	To what extent did you feel proud, confident or self-assured?	
7	To what extent did you feel interested, attentive or curious?	
8	To what extent did you feel grateful or appreciative?	
9	To what extent did you feel inspired?	
10	To what extent did you feel hopeful, optimistic or encouraged?	

Add up the scores of the pleasant emotions. You can try this again at the end of the book to see whether there is an improvement. The combined scores can be interpreted as follows:

- Total 0–5: A low score: There is a reasonable chance you may be dealing with a depression. Alternative, something truly awful happened today, which means this is only a snapshot. If you find that you are experiencing prolonged feelings of sadness or gloom, we recommend that you contact your GP before continuing this book.
- Total 6–15: A somewhat low score: There is substantial room for personal growth and positive development.
- Total 16–29: A fairly high score: There is room to reinforce and improve the positive aspects of your life.
- Total 30–40: A high score: You experienced a very positive 24 hours.

Which emotions do you experience less or more strongly? Is that something you recognize? Can you determine why you experience some pleasant emotions to a lesser degree? You should realize that this in only a snapshot. It is a good idea to fill in the questionnaire every day for a week, for example, before you fill in the diary from Exercise 1 (on page 17). That will provide you with an even better insight into how often you experience pleasant emotions.

Exercise 3: The '3 good things-exercise'

Make a habit of visualizing positive experiences. Using this core exercise from positive psychology, you can improve your ability to bask in the (after)glow of positive and pleasant experiences. You can perform the following exercise every day this coming week. A good time for it would be in bed, just before lights out; or while celebrating the end of the day over drinks with your partner.

Review your day, and take a moment to appreciate three positive experiences. What good things happened to you today? When did you experience one of the positive emotions, such as love, pride, inspiration, hope, interest, calm, or joy? It could be that you saw something wonderful; it could be that you enjoyed something; it could be that you freed up some time for the little things that make you happy. Even if you have had a hard day or if you are going through a rough patch, this is a good exercise to do. You will nearly always find some little positive event or experience. Taking the time to appreciate these experiences is a worthwhile thing. Consider each experience. Try to visualize and experience the events. Enjoy them. Try to make this a habit.

Exercise 4: Write about positive memories

Another way to experience pleasant emotions is by writing about very positive memories. Can you remember a moment when you felt one of the ten pleasant emotions very strongly?

19

Try to remember joy, calmness, or love; a time when you had a major crush on someone, perhaps, or felt intensely loved or in love; a time when you felt moved by a piece of writing or music; a time when you created something. Take ten to twenty minutes every evening to write about those moments in your life. Try to visualize them: What happened? Who were you with? Where were you? How did you feel? What did the experience mean to you? Limit your writing sessions, for example, one memory every evening – this will help you make sure it remains a fun thing to do.

Exercise 5: Positive focus

Resolve to pay attention to positive things for at least fifteen minutes during your next active undertaking (taking a walk, riding a bike). Focus your attention on the pleasant things you encounter, such as the sounds of laughter or birdsong, the colours of flowers in bloom, dogs at play, clouds moving across the sky, fragrant scents. As soon as you notice you are beginning to note negative aspects (littered streets, a pungent stench, people shouting or yelling, etc.) or that your thoughts are turning inward, recognize this fact and refocus on the pleasant things that surround you.

Exercise 6: The little things

One of the founders of positive psychology is Chris Peterson. He said:

For the first part of my adult life, I did not have time for the small things which I knew would make me happy: 'There will be time for that later'. I was fortunate enough to realise at a certain point that I would never have time, unless I made time. That is when the rest of my life began.

- Is there something that moves you?
- What takes up most of your time?
- What goal are you chasing?

- What are your 'little things that make you happy'?
- How much time do you free up for these things?
- What is already there for you to enjoy?

Exercise 7: Appreciate what is there

One way of enhancing pleasant emotions is to become and remain aware of the things you are grateful for. We human beings tend to focus a lot of our attention on what is not there, on what is missing. If there is anything that is guaranteed to reinforce and increase unpleasant emotions, it is that. Becoming and remaining unhappy or dissatisfied is actually very easy to do. There is always something that is not perfect in our lives, or is missing from it. We get used so easily to the material things, to running water, to a lovely view, to anything that is good. And high expectations are also an excellent breeding ground for disappointment and unhappiness.

Being satisfied can actually be much harder. Part of positive living is to appreciate and be grateful for all the valuable things in your life. During these next few weeks, try to be grateful for what you have in your day-to-day life. Make sure you do so regularly. Make a good start to the day when you get out of bed. Be grateful for something, even if it is no more than being alive, breathing, with another day at your fingertips. Or consider your life during a walk, while you wait for a bus, when you are on the train. Take a moment, and look around. What do you see? What do you see that surprises you? What leaves you amazed? Doing this exercise every day might be too much of a good thing, but at least if you make a regular feature of your life, it will certainly leave a lasting impression.

Exercise 8: Reverse a negative situation

Try to be grateful even at times when you are in a negative mood, for example, if you are restless, if you are having a moan, or if you are grumbling to people around you.

Begin by noticing and recognizing your unhappiness, your dissatisfaction, your complaining. Then, consider what is causing you to feel this way. Were you expecting a certain outcome? Do you have a need that is not being fulfilled? Take a moment to contemplate your feelings and their causes. This can help you to voice your expectations, needs, and disappointments. Chapter 7, on communicating, examines this in greater detail.

Once you have noticed and recognized the situation and the emotions it is causing you to feel, another useful tool is to ask yourself: Which good aspects are there to this situation? Define the things you can be grateful for to help you reverse a negative situation without wallowing in or repressing unpleasant emotions.

Last week, Laura visited her parents-in-law along with her two kids. Her husband had gone away for the week. Laura has a good relationship with her parents-in-law, but she was feeling grumpy on Saturday morning. The kids were more excitable than usual, and Laura did not feel her parents-in-law were handling this very well. She took a moment to recognize the fact that she was grumbling and upset. She found that she was a little fed up with her husband being out of town on account of his work, and that so much extra weight rested on her shoulders as a result. She allowed herself to feel this way, and then decided to discuss it with her husband sometime next week. She knew it was all part of his job, but he had been gone quite often during the past several months. It might be possible for him to take this into account. Having voiced her resolve, she was able to feel grateful for being able to stay with her parents-in-law that weekend, and for the fact that they had made time and opened up their house for her and her kids. This let her view the weekend in a brand-new light.

Note

1   Based on Fredrickson, 2009; p. 56.

References

Bryant, F.B., and Veroff, J. (2007). *Savoring: A new model of positive experiences*. Mahwah NJ: Lawrence Erlbaum.

Fredrickson, B.L. (2009). *Positivity*. New York: Three Rivers Press.

Hayes, S.C., Strosahl, K.D., Wilson, K.G., Bisset, R.T., Pistorello, J., Toarmino, D., Polusny, M.A., Dykstra, T.A., Batten, S.V., Bergan, J., Stewart, S.H., Zvolensky, M.J., Eifert, G.H., Bond, F.W., Forsyth, J.P., Karekla, M., and McCurry, S.M. (2004). Measuring experiential avoidance: a preliminary test of a working model. *The Psychological Record, 54,* 553–578.

Chapter 2

Enjoy your talent

Introduction

'Be yourself.' We hear it often, and it is an appealing idea. Being yourself seems to be an important condition for personal growth. In the field of humanist psychology, 'being yourself' takes centre stage. According to this school of thought, a safe environment, attention, and unconditional love are important prerequisites to developing yourself in a way that suits you. Positive psychology uses humanist psychology as part of its foundation, with regards to creating conditions enabling personal growth. One of the latest insights is concerned with developing and using the strengths and qualities present in each of us. The studies discussed below demonstrate that this course of action leads to growth and happiness. This chapter explains why that would be the case. The exercises invite you to consider your strengths and qualities, as a prelude to building on them in Chapter 3.

Basic needs and motivation

Each of us has their strong suits. Some of us are patient; others are quick to act. Some are decisive; others are good at listening. In the field of positive psychology there are different ways of paying attention to how we use our own strengths. Peterson and Seligman (2004), for example, developed a model of character strengths. Examples of character strengths include courage, wisdom or friendliness. Another approach has been developed by psychologist Alex Linley and his colleagues (Linley et al., 2010). They view strengths from a wider perspective, in the form of the things you are good at, and which you enjoy doing. This chapter mainly uses this latter definition. Using your strengths leads to a positive motivation for self-development, encouraging you to aim for and achieve meaningful goals. We will first explain this using the theory of self-determination which provides context as to why people do what it is they do.

The theory of self-determination and the three basic needs

One of the most influential theories in positive psychology is that of self-determination, developed by Ryan and Deci (2000). Self-determination means acting based on psychological freedom instead of coercion. This theory states that people have three basic needs, and that meeting these needs is important to a person's performance and growth. These needs are: experiencing competence, autonomy, and connectedness.

The need to experience competence means that people wish to feel capable, to feel that they are doing something well. You want to feel that the skills you command are required to achieve certain results. You want to be able to successfully complete certain challenges. The need for autonomy is experiencing a certain degree of independence. You want to be able to make your own choices, to provide direction to your own life. You do not want others to determine what you should and should not be doing. This need is concerned with experiencing freedom of thought and action. The need for connectedness means having meaningful relationships. It means having other people you can trust, people with whom you can share your personal experiences. It is the need to be part of a community, to belong, to be accepted.

Motivation

The theory of self-determination provides a global definition of two different types of motivation: extrinsic motivation and intrinsic motivation. Extrinsic motivation involves experiencing a certain degree of force, of 'having to'. This type of motivation is the result of an outside force; your actions as a result are motivated by the possibility of being rewarded or punished. Or you feel pressured into doing something because you feel obligated to do so; avoiding it would cause you to feel shame. Activities born from extrinsic motivation are more prone to causing stress. Intrinsic motivation, on the other hand, involves action from your own interest and the joy that you feel in the activity itself. This is 'wanting to' instead of 'having to'. You feel a sense of satisfaction in performing the activities themselves because they are pleasant, or because they fit your values, and contribute to realizing the goals you have set for yourself. These goals are relevant and meaningful to you, and have not been forced upon you by an outside agent. The activities lead you to feel mainly joyous, free, and alive.

The theory of self-determination predicts that, when our three basic needs are met, we are more prone to act on the basis of intrinsic motivation – and vice versa: the more we act from intrinsic motivation, the more our basic needs are met.

Research shows that pursuing goals based on intrinsic motivation has a number of positive effects (Sheldon and Elliot, 1999). For one thing, it positively affects our dedication and determination; we try better, perform harder, and are less quick to abandon a task. This increases the chances that we meet our goals. In addition, we feel more satisfied when we achieve goals of our own choosing rather than goals based on outside expectations. When we are intrinsically motivated, we experience a greater sense of well-being, greater joy in our actions, greater success, and greater satisfaction with the results we achieve. All in all, we experience more pleasant emotions! You can also imagine that your confidence in your competences increases when you take part in activities based on intrinsic motivation. You enter a positive spiral: your autonomy grows based on your increasing confidence in your abilities, which likely encourages you to undertake new challenges. This is how you achieve personal growth and development. Once you gain insight into which activities give you joy, and which goals you feel are important to pursue, you can get into a 'flow' (the subject of Chapter 3).

Strengths, learned behaviours and weaknesses

Psychologist Alex Linley studies the relationship between using our strengths and experiencing well-being. Linley distinguishes four different types of skills: strengths, unrealized strengths, learned behaviours, and weaknesses.

Strengths are skills and qualities you use in everyday life, and which give you a sense of joy and energy to apply. It is important to recognize which activities let you experience joy, passion, and interest, and what skills you are applying at that time. These are your strengths. The more you apply them in your life, the more energized you will feel, and the greater your chances of entering the positive spiral mentioned previously. Strengths can also be hidden, as a result of being hardly or never used. In that case, your strengths have not yet been realized. There is a real opportunity for personal growth and well-being to be had here, since you feel even more energized once you develop these skills. Say, for example, that you are highly creative, but were never encouraged to develop your creativity during your childhood. This means your creativity is present in potential only, and could be a resource for you to develop.

Linley made an important discovery, namely that not everything we are good at is necessarily a strength. This is quite an eye-opener to many people. We can excel at certain behaviours which do not, in fact, let us experience any particular sense of enjoyment or vitality when we apply them. Linley terms these skills 'learned behaviours'; behaviours which were emphasized during our childhood, which we were encouraged to developed, and which other people frequently complimented us on. These are behaviours we practised frequently, and have come to excel at. Linley found that these behaviours can actually drain energy instead of providing it, leading to a reduced sense of well-being in the long term. The difference between a strength and a learned behaviour, in other words, mainly lies in the degree to which you find it enjoyable and energizing to use. Someone else may not notice the difference between the two by looking at you, because you are good at both your strengths and your learned behaviours – even if your learned behaviours actually take an effort and drains your energy levels. You may be part of an organization that calls upon your learned behaviours time and again – these are things you are very good at, but which only drain your energy. As a result, you will most likely fade instead of flourish. Linley advises us to restrict the degree to which we use learned behaviours, creating room for the development and use of our strengths. The exercises discuss how to do this in greater detail.

Finally, Linley provides another important insight: our culture has come to place heavy emphasis on reducing weaknesses, even though emphasizing these aspects of our skillset is harmful to our sense of well-being. Weaknesses are behaviours we are not so good at, and which it is hard for us to properly acquire. Using an extraordinary effort, we may be able to, but we will never excel at them, and they will certainly never give us any sense of joy. Think of teaching someone who is tone deaf to play the piano. You may be able to teach them how to read sheet music and play a little ditty, but that would be about the best you could hope for. Each one of us has our own strengths and weaknesses. This simple fact means that we are all unique. Linley emphasizes the importance of accepting our weaknesses and of avoiding the expenditure of too much energy in pursuit of these behaviours. That way, we can free up the energy we need to address the use and development of our (unrealized) strengths. By paying attention to the strengths we have not yet realized, we can reach a positive spiral.

In summary:

- *Strengths*: behaviours you are good at, and which give you energy. You are recommended to use (and keep using) them. If you keep making more use of your strengths in your life, you will arrive at those activities that suit you and that you enjoy.
- *Unrealized strengths*: behaviours you have not yet developed, but which you could come to master, and which would give you energy. You are recommended to discover and develop these strengths. They contribute to your personal development and well-being.
- *Learned behaviours*: things you excel at as a result of having practised them often, but which do not give you energy. You are recommended to apply these behaviours only in moderation, since they can lead you to exhaust yourself.
- *Weaknesses*: things that others may excel at, but you simply do not. You are recommended to look for possibilities in your life which do not involve the use of your weaknesses, and not to focus on them. The energy you free up by turning away from your weaknesses is better used to apply and develop your (unrealized) strengths.

Scientific research (Linley et al., 2010) into the effects of the advice given above is best summarized as follows:

People who make more use of their strengths and less use of their learned behaviours and weaknesses:

- Are happier;
- Have greater self-confidence and self-esteem;
- Have more energy and vitality;
- Experience less stress;
- Are more resilient;
- More often achieve their goals;
- Perform better at work;
- Are more involved in their work; and
- Experience greater personal growth and development.

As early as the first century AD, the philosopher Epictetus described how people can assume a role in their life which is not compatible with their strengths. This means they are not doing what they do best, which is a true loss:

> If, in a play, you assume a role that is above your ability, then you will not only have failed in your performance, but will also have missed out on the role you would have been able to perform. (Epictetus 2011, p. 51)

Shifting the focus from weaknesses to strengths

It comes as no surprise that most people find it easier to indicate their weaknesses rather than their strengths. We are simply confronted with the former more frequently than the latter – because our schools, our society, many organizations and educational institutions are focused on mitigating our weaknesses and vulnerabilities. Recognizing and wielding your strengths as part of your work or education is not a given. If things go wrong, we begin to analyse them. We look for failings in people's performances. Plans for improvement are implemented to help reduce these weaknesses by additional schooling and training. This fails to take into account the effort required, and the resulting lack of enjoyment or satisfaction.

People blossom when the focus in their education and work is shifted instead to their strengths, and when organizations try to make maximum use of people's strengths by, for example, matching employees who complement each other based on their strengths. Companies that act in this manner encounter less absenteeism, and increased team effectiveness.

But there is another reason why we have difficulty with defining our strengths, which is that we are used to being critical of ourselves. To us, our personal qualities are 'normal'; even natural. It is hard for us to take pride in something we are good at, and to recognize the skills that let us do something well. It may be because a sense of modesty has been such a big part of our upbringing, or having a critical eye is ingrained in our culture, but it is more likely the result of an important survival strategy, which has forced us to keep improving. Our current society has less use for such a self-critical attitudes. Nevertheless, many of us suffer the comments of an inner critic, constructed from our memories of a demanding parent or teacher.

Many people find it hard to recognize, appreciate, or encourage their own talents and capabilities. And because many of us are so familiar with our own modesty and weaknesses, making those weaknesses the focus of our attention and improvement may have come to feel like the safer option. Experience teaches us that many people find it a frightening prospect to fully acknowledge their strengths. The same may be true for you yourself.

This process is excellently put into words in a text by Marianne Williamson (1992), cited as a quote by Nelson Mandela:

> Our deepest fear is not that we are inadequate. Our deepest fear is that we are powerful beyond measure. It is our light, not our darkness that most frightens us. We ask ourselves, who am I to be brilliant, gorgeous, talented, fabulous? Actually, who are you not to be? You are a child of God. Your playing small does not serve the world. There is nothing enlightened about shrinking so that other people won't feel insecure around you. We are all meant to shine, as children do. We were born to make manifest the glory of God that is within us. It's not just in some of us; it's in everyone. And as we let our own light shine, we unconsciously give other people permission to do the same. As we are liberated from our own fear, our presence automatically liberates others.

Get to work on your strengths!

Recognizing and utilizing your strengths is an important part of leading a positive life. Do what it is that you are good at, and you will feel joy. You trigger a positive spiral which helps you reinforce your confidence and joy in learning and applying skills that suit your talents and strengths. This does take a certain amount of courage: Putting yourself out there, challenging yourself. Negative motivation may lead you to play it safe, to rely on routine and on learned behaviours: 'I had better stick to what I know; even at the cost of some enjoyment. No crazy adventures or silliness.' Extrinsic motivation, for example, may lead you to strive for recognition, to boost your self-image, or to attain a certain status.

The following exercises are aimed at discovering and concretizing your strengths. The following chapter, about flow (see page 49), explains how to apply this in practice.

Using and developing strengths – exercises

The first exercise lets you map your strengths. This is followed by a number of exercises and questions designed to help you in discovering the other strengths you may have overlooked.

Lastly, you formulate and define your most important strengths. The introduction mentioned that you do not necessarily have to complete all the exercises in every chapter, but you should note that the exercises in this chapter do follow a particular structure. This makes it important that you, at least, complete the exercises in the order in which they are given.

Exercise 1: Overview of strengths and learned behaviours

The following is an (alphabetical) overview of personal strengths, with brief descriptions and (near) synonyms. This overview is based on Linley et al. (2010).[1]

Step 1

First, read through this list at your leisure. All you have to do is place a cross in the third column for the strengths that you feel apply to you.

Step 2

Once you have finished, have a look at the strengths you have checked. Now use the fourth column to select those properties and characteristics that provide you with a sense of enjoyment or energy when you use them actively.

This is your first overview of and distinction between your strengths and learned behaviours.

Table 2.1 Strengths: Overview

Strengths	Properties and characteristics	Applies to me	Energy and enjoyment
Adaptable	You are able to properly react to changes, and letting go of them where necessary. *Flexible, improvisation skills, converting, accommodating, pliable.*		
Adventurous	You dare to take the road less travelled, to take risks, and to think outside the box. *Entrepreneurial, discovering, trying.*		
Attentive	You have all your wits about you. You can always pinpoint the essence of what someone else is talking about. *Thoughtful, present.*		
Authentic	You remain who you are; you act based on your values, even in the face of difficulty. *Sincere, original, honest, true, reliable, spontaneous, candid.*		
Competitive	You challenge others; you do not shy away from conflict. You want to be the best. *Combative, winner's mentality.*		

Table 2.1 continued

Strengths	Properties and characteristics	Applies to me	Energy and enjoyment
Courageous	You are able to act and decide, despite any concerns or fears these actions or decisions might inspire. *Brave, fearless, gutsy, heroic.*		
Creative	You come up with new products, ideas, combinations. *Artistic, original.*		
Curious	You are interested in what is new, and are keen to work out how things work. *Interested, attentive, in the know.*		
Decisive	You are able to act quickly and adequately. *Action-oriented, resolute, diligent, enthusiastic.*		
Driven	You are strongly motivated to achieve. *Enthusiastic, go-getter, decisive, ambitious, impassioned, dedicated, incisive.*		
Efficient	You are always able to make the best possible use of your time. *Expedient, quick, short and sweet.*		
Emotionally intelligent	You can quickly determine the emotions you and others are feeling. *Sensitive, susceptible, empathic, self-aware.*		
Empathic	You understand how other people think and act, and you recognise their pains and limitations. You can see things from someone else's perspective. *Compassionate, understanding, sympathetic.*		

Table 2.1 continued

Enlightening	You are able to simplify and clearly explain matters. *Explaining, conveying, providing insight.*		
Ethical	You have a strongly developed sense of morality, and act based on what you think is right or wrong. *Moral, morally-philosophical.*		
Eye for detail	You pay attention to detail; you are not satisfied until everything is as it should be. *Careful, precise, astute.*		
Eye for improvement	You can always find opportunities to improve processes and products. *Optimising, perfecting, proceeding.*		
Growth-oriented	You are strongly motivated towards self-development, and are always able to identify opportunities for that purpose. *Eager to learn, feedback-oriented.*		
Harmonious	You always remain calm; even in difficult situations you remain confident of yourself. *Stable, balanced, calm, sensible, confident, sombre.*		
Helpful	You are always there to help; you are good at supporting others. *Service-oriented, collegial, caring, selfless.*		
Humorous	You have an eye for the funny side of any situation, allowing you to put things into perspective and to make people laugh. *Comical, funny, playful, witty.*		

Table 2.1 continued

Strengths	Properties and characteristics	Applies to me	Energy and enjoyment
Innovative	You can always find new options, approaches and solutions. *Inventive, imaginative, improvisational skills, pioneering.*		
Inspiring	You are always able to provide others with new momentum and motivate them to act and participate. *Stimulating, encouraging, motivating.*		
Judiciousness	You are able to quickly assess matters and make decisions. *Decisive, defining.*		
Modest	You take a back seat and recognise others' contributions to success. *Straightforward, discrete, unobtrusive.*		
Optimistic	You always see possibilities; you have a positive mind-set. *Opportunity-based thinking, self-confidence, cheerful.*		
Orderly	You have a place for everything, and everything in its place. *Systematic, structured, ordered, neat, proper.*		
Organisationally capable	You are able to bring people and things together in time. *Steering, managing, achieving, coordinating.*		
Patient	You are able to give things their due time. *Open, receptive, steady.*		

Table 2.1 continued

Persistent	You keep your sights on an end result, and do not allow adversity to stand in your way. *Endurance, perseverance.*		
Persuasive	You are good at making others see things your way. *Convincing, persuading.*		
Reflective	You think things through and consider relevant meanings and consequences. *Consider, review, ponder.*		
Relationship-oriented	You find it easy to reach out to others and are good at building up and reinforcing relationships. *Inter-personal skills, involvement, thoughtful, friendly, involved.*		
Relaxed	You are able to be relaxed and at peace. *Airiness, detachment, relaxedness, carefreeness.*		
Resilient	You are quick to recover from adversity and let it challenge you to reach new heights. *Stress-resistant, stable, resilience, strong-willed.*		
Resolving power	You are good at solving problems. *Demystifying, untangling.*		
Responsible	You support what you say and do; you are always willing and able to account for yourself; you keep to your agreements. *Disciplined, serious.*		
Result-oriented	You have a clear view of the end product and steer towards achieving that. *Execution and outcome-oriented, business-like.*		

Table 2.1 continued

Strengths	Properties and characteristics	Applies to me	Energy and enjoyment
Righteous	You are keen to make sure all parties involved are treated equally. *Eye for equality, honesty.*		
Self-reliant	You take care of yourself. *Self-reliant, autonomous.*		
Storytelling	You are able to craft information into stories which you are able to compellingly convey. *Imaginative, enlivening, making relevant.*		
Strategical	You have an eye for existing interests, alliances and win-win situations. *Bridge-builder, tactician.*		
Supportive	You always find opportunities to help others and to be of service. *Assisting, mobilizing.*		
Systematic	You go about matters systematically, step-by-step. *Measure twice cut once, reflecting.*		
Visionary	You are skilled at anticipating potential problems and taking action to prevent these problems from occurring. *Anticipating, pioneering, preventing.*		
Visionary	You have an eye for meaningful long-term developments and possibilities. *Future-oriented, mission.*		
Writing Skills	You are able to phrase things on paper systematically or understandably.		

Exercise 2: Discover your strengths[2]

The following is a list of questions that can help you discover your strengths. Take your time to answer each of them. If you cannot think of an answer, move on to the next question. You can always return to a question you initially left blank once you complete the list for the first time.

Question 1

What was something you could be fully engrossed in when you were a child? What could you keep doing without stopping; what toy did you never want to put down? Is there something you used to do when you were younger, but which you have become far better at? You can ask your parents or other people who knew you well as a child to help you answer these questions.

Question 2

What situations and activities put you right in your comfort zone, making you lose track of time? What activities give you energy; what do you look forward to? Think of your work, but also how you spend your free time.

Question 3

What are or were the things you find or found it easy to take up? What comes or came to you with practically no effort?

Question 4

What were the best compliments you ever received?

Question 5

What makes you enthusiastic; what are you passionate about? What puts colour on your cheeks; what makes you sound alive? Feel free to ask other people who know you well.

Question 6

You are given the chance to work in a job of your choice for a company of your choice for a year. It can be a job with room for development, and which includes training opportunities. It is a paid job. Where would you want to work, and what would you want to do during the year?

Question 7

Who are sources of inspiration to you?

Question 8

What do you consider to be your parents' strengths and weaknesses?

Question 9

.During what period of your life and career were you the happiest?

Question 10

During what period of your life and career were you forced to deal with adversity?

Exercise 3: Discover your strengths, continued

Have a look at what you wrote down in Exercise 2. Which qualities present themselves? Write those down in the right column of the table below. You can also use the list from Exercise 1 by way of memory aid or checklist. Remember: Strengths are skills and/or qualities that give you enjoyment and energy.

Table 2.2 Strengths and qualities

1. Which strengths present themselves? *Keep in mind that some strengths may be very early to manifest.*	
2. Which strengths do you apply at those times? *Being engrossed in an activity is often the sign of a strength at work!*	
3. Which strengths did you develop there? *Effortless learning is often an indication of a strength.*	
4. Did this compliment refer to one of your strengths? *Other people often pick up on your strengths.*	
5. Is this where your strengths make themselves known? *The things you are passionate about are often indicative of your strengths.*	
6. Which of your strengths can you apply in your dream job? *Use your imagination; which strengths does your dream job address?*	
7. What are their strengths? *Are some of them the same as yours?*	
8. Which strengths did they pass on to you? *Some strengths are genetically determined.*	
9. Which strengths were you able to address during that time? *Periods of happiness often allow you to fully apply your strengths.*	
10. Which strengths did you apply to help you through? *Periods of adversity may uncover strengths you had not yet realized existed.*	

Exercise 4: Other people's thoughts

Ask several people around you to join you in this journey of discovery. Give a copy of the overview of your strengths from Exercise 1 to 3, to five of them. Ask them to select the five qualities they most identify with you. If they ask, you can tell them it is part of a training exercise to increase your inspiration or job satisfaction.

Their second assignment is to provide concrete examples of each of the qualities they selected; these would be examples where they saw you applying that strength.

Discuss the answers with your helpers. The goal is to engage in a conversation that will leave you with an increased insight into your strengths. Your mission is:

- To listen carefully, and to thoroughly consider their responses.
- To keep asking questions if you are uncertain of the answers. You may feel this is immodest, but it is not. You want to make everything as explicit as possible. If others identify a strength that you do not immediately recognize, then that is actually very interesting.
- To thank your helpers for their time and effort, and for compliments they have given.

Tip: Who to choose?

- The most fruitful results are obtained by using an eclectic mix of helpers. Think of asking your partner, a good friend, a neighbour, a family member or a colleague.
- Consider asking a manager or superior. This may seem a little daunting, but it can be the start of a conversation about what you consider to be your strengths. The next chapter covers how to set up a career context which allows you to make the best possible use of your strengths. This is easiest and most productive if your superior is willing to help you out. Involving them in this exercise opens the door to that scenario.

- Consider asking at least one person you are not intimate or close with. People who tend to view you from more of a distance can come up with some very interesting answers.

You can copy the following page (feedback form) from this book and give them to your intended helpers.

Strengths: Feedback form

First, I would like to thank you for taking the time to provide me with feedback regarding my strengths.

Here is a list of possible strengths. Could you please indicate five strengths that you most associate with me? You can fill them in below. Could you also give a concrete example for each of these strengths? I am looking for examples where you saw me demonstrate each particular strength, and what it is you saw me doing at the time. If you cannot find one or more of the strengths you are looking for in the list, please feel free to describe them in your own words.

I would very much like to ask you about your answers in a follow-up interview.

Table 2.3 Feedback form

Strengths	Example situations and actions/behaviours
1.	
2.	
3.	
4.	
5.	

Once you have received feedback from all of your helpers, compare the feedback forms. Which of the strengths have they mentioned more than once? Are there any strengths there that you had not considered, but which are recognizable and appealing to you? Write down the most important and appealing strengths in the following summary table, and indicate whether applying these strengths provides you with a sense of enjoyment and energy.

Table 2.4 Strengths: Summary table

Mentioned more than once	Applying this makes me feel joyous/energized

Exercise 5: Edit your overview of strengths

Completing Exercise 1 provided you with an overview of your strengths based on an existing list. Exercises 2 and 3 involved looking at your life creatively, and may have led you to uncover new strengths. Exercise 4 resulted in an inventory of strengths that other people feel apply to you.

Compare the results of these exercises. It may be that you have gained new insight into your strengths. You may have found a description of a strength that combined several behaviours into a more appropriate, all-encompassing definition – or you may have been able to make a specific strengths more explicit.

What do you now consider to be your five most important strengths – strengths whose application gives you energy and enjoyment?

Table 2.5 Strengths: Top five

My five most important strengths	Description of this strength in my own words
1.	
2.	
3.	
4.	
5.	

For the coming days, keep an eye out for how and when these strengths manifest in your life (at work, at home, during time off, during studies). The next chapter will provide you with practical means of applying these insights. The following exercise is the first step in this process.

Exercise 6: Make use of strengths during difficult situations

What hard or difficult situation are you currently faced with in your life? It can be part of your private life or your career. It may have started some time ago; it may have developed only recently. It can be something major you are trying to cope with; it can be something small but slightly bothersome. Now take a look at your list of strengths. Start with the ones from Exercise 5. But you can also take a look at the strengths you initially indicated in Exercise 1. Which of the strengths, which you may or may not already be using in the situation, could be of value in dealing with it? Write down what this application could look like: A strategy for dealing with the situation using your strength. Use this strategy during the coming week. What do you notice?

Notes

1   With kind permission from the author.
2   Based on an exercise in *Talentenwijzer* by Djoerd Hiemstra (2011).

References

Epictetus (2011). *Zakboekje: wenken voor een evenwichtig leven.* Amsterdam: Boom uitgevers Amsterdam.

Hiemstra, D. (2011). *Talentenwijzer: Talentontwikkelingsprogramma. (Talent development program).* Den Haag: BoomLemma.

Linley, A., Willars, J., and Biswas-Diener, R. (2010). *The strengths book: Be confident, be successful, and enjoy better relationships by realising the best of you.* Coventry: Capp Press.

Peterson, C., and Seligman, M.E.P. (2004). *Character strengths and virtues: A handbook and classification.* New York: Oxford University Press.

Ryan, R.M., and Deci, E.L. (2000). Self-determination theory and the facilitation of intrinsic motivation, social development, and well-being. *American Psychologist, 55*, 68–78.

Sheldon, K.M., and Elliot, A.J. (1999). Goal striving, need satisfaction, and longitudinal well-being; The self-concordance model. *Journal of Personality and Social Psychology, 76*, 482–497.

Williamson, M. (1992). *A return to love: Reflections on the principles of* A Course in Miracles. New York: HarperCollins Publishers.

Chapter 3

Lose yourself

Introduction

Is it not one of life's tragedies that we can be our own worst enemies? That our self-awareness tires us out? We keep wondering whether we are adequate, whether we are failing, how we come across. We scrutinize other people's responses to use for signs of rejection. Psychologists talk about 'self-preoccupation': We are completely absorbed with ourselves. One of the most important features of this preoccupation is that we worry. We can be ever so darn critical of ourselves, reviewing our own performance in the context of high standards and norms. People prone to fearfulness or depression are often even more susceptible to this. Our self-preoccupation is a barrier that stands in the way of a positive, satisfying life. How do we deal with it? Worry, self-criticism; these cannot be switched off by pressing a button. Attempting to suppress them is counterproductive.

One potent remedy lies in developing self-respect and compassion. This will be the focus of Chapter 5. In the current chapter, we focus on learning how to lose ourselves in our daily activities; in a sense, forgetting about ourselves. This leads to a more joyous life, because the attention shifts away from the self to focus on the experience instead.

Losing yourself in your daily life

Hungarian psychologist Mihály Csíkszentmihályi is one of the founders of positive psychology along with Martin Seligman. Csíkszentmihályi studied the way people experience their daily lives and work, and developed the theory of 'flow' (2001) based on his findings. Alternatively known as the 'zone', this theory offers a handhold for increasing the joy and energy we have and feel in our life and work. Csíkszentmihályi and his assistants conducted thousands of interviews with varied and various people about their daily lives. Based on these interviews, he found that many people find it difficult to truly enjoy their daily activities, and to experience them as truly satisfying. There can be numerous reasons for this, and here are a few:

- Focusing on the result instead of the process. Athletes, for example, can enjoy the game and the conflict with an opponent (process). But they can also be overly focused on winning and achieving a certain ranking (result). If the drive focuses on the result, then this produces a different energy than when it focuses on the actions themselves.
- Working according to a routine instead of looking for challenges. Routines provide a sense of safety. They operate on the basis of what is established because letting go of security can be frightening. This is why many people become caught up in a job they do not like, for example, because they are concerned about risking their monthly income.
- Being insecure or afraid of criticism. This leads to a continuous fear of failure and error. Doubt and uncertainty are paralytics.
- Acting from an extrinsic motivation. This was covered in Chapter 2. People can feel they need to act a certain way to meet others' expectations, instead of acting from their own intrinsic motivation.
- Not being present in the moment. People sometimes do certain things while simultaneously worrying about other matters.

To illustrate this last point, have a look at the example of Eric:

Eric works as a teacher at a primary school. He enjoys reading stories to the children. It relaxes him, and he enjoys the captivated looks on the children's faces as they listen. Eric knows he excels in conveying excitement. But this week, he is not able to keep his attention on his storytelling, resulting in a restless group of kids. They can tell Eric is distracted. What is going on? Eric's has been trying to sell his house for a while now. He had an interested buyer a couple of days ago, but it is beginning to look like they will not be able to successfully conclude the negotiations. Eric is worried about his financial situation. While he is reading to the children, this worry seeps into his consciousness – leading to an inner unrest. This unrest disrupts the interaction between story-telling and captivated listening.

You will probably be familiar with this type of situation. Many people find it hard to enjoy day-to-day activities if they are aware of and distracted by other matters (worries, uncertainties, doubts, self-preoccupations), preventing them from living in the moment.

Csíkszentmihályi also found something else during his interviews. Hundreds of interviewees indicated that they felt joy every day, and these people notably all indicated the same characteristics. These characteristics were: having a clear goal and attaching importance to that goal, indicating intrinsic motivation. The interviewees indicated that they were so absorbed by the activities that they had no room for worry. They were so fully focused on the activity itself that the result of that activity became of secondary importance. Their level of concentration led them to 'forget themselves', as it were. Csíkszentmihályi defined this as an optimal experience, which he termed 'flow'.

The 'flow' state (or 'being in the zone') means that someone is fully absorbed in their current activity, including all information resent in their consciousness related to and in conformity with the goals. This enables an effortless flow of energy, leading a person to enjoy the execution of the activity. Csíkszentmihályi also discovered that flow is not dependent on education, age, or social standing. He describes, for example, flow as experienced by a factory worker, by a young female lawyer, and by a mother. The factory worker stood at a conveyor belt, and had to perform the same acts hundreds of times a day. He had been doing this for five years, and had been enjoying every minute of it. He had turned his process of improvement into a sport, becoming more and more efficient so as to keep exceeding his personal best. The young lawyer was tasked with looking for background information used in various cases. She spent full days in the library in search of the literature required to support certain arguments. The mother took pleasure in reading to her young daughter; something they both enjoyed. The mother was fully absorbed by those moments.

According to Csíkszentmihályi (2001, p. 75) people who regularly experience flow and the joy it brings, defined flow by the following characteristics:

1. Flow is experienced when we perform a task which we know we can successfully complete;
2. We need to be able to focus on the activity;
3. We are able to retain the focus because there are clear, concrete goals to the task;
4. The task is subject to clear feedback: We receive information which indicates whether we are reaching our goals;
5. We are intensely but effortlessly engaged, meaning we are not distracted by everyday worries or disappointments;
6. While we are executing the task, we feel completely in control;
7. We are completely unaware of our self while performing the activity; but once it is completed, we do feel our self-awareness has been expanded; and
8. Our perception of time is altered. Sometimes, the hours seem to fly by. Sometimes, a moment seems to last ages.

Flow is most easily triggered when you are facing a challenge which demands certain skills. These are skills that tie in to your strengths, the strengths you investigated in the previous chapter. It is critical that the activity is not performed with a view to some future reward, but because the experience itself is satisfying and enjoyable. It is the process of performing an act that is important, not the result of that act. The result is of secondary importance. Csíkszentmihályi calls these experiences 'autotelic' ('auto' meaning 'self', 'telos' meaning 'goal'). Here are three examples illustrating the concept:

If you teach children because you want them to be good citizens, and to be able to obtain a good societal standing, then that is not an autotelic activity – you are focused on the eventual result, not on the activity itself. If you teach children because it gives you joy to work with kids, then that same activity is now autotelic.

If you are a politician with the goal of attaining power of bringing about a more perfect society, then that is not an autotelic activity – your primary focus is on your results. A politician who enjoys developing and debating their vision, on the other hand, is engaged in an autotelic activity.

Designing your garden to impress your friends is not autotelic – your main concern is what others will think of the result. Maintaining your garden because you enjoy sowing, cutting, and fertilizing is autotelic.

Introducing flow into your life

Flow is introduced into your life by creating challenges that inspire you, and that tie in with your strengths. Be it work, spare time, sports, games, or family life – the most important thing is to balance the challenge with your skills. The challenge has to tie in with your skills as to bring about the experience of flow. You cannot experience flow if something comes too easily to you – not having to put in an effort or concentrate frees up mental room. This unoccupied space is easily filled up with unwanted worries or concerns once your mind starts wondering. Alternatively, you cannot experience flow if something is too hard – it will only frustrate you. As a result, you become self-conscious; you worry about your abilities; you become afraid to fail.

In addition, you need to be free in your choice of activity, and you need to be intrinsically motivated. It is much more difficult to experience flow during an activity you are ordered to do. Nevertheless, it may be possible to develop a taste for it as you are working, if you are able to view the assigned task as an interesting challenge for yourself. Lastly, it is important that there are clear and concrete targets, and that there are clear criteria for feedback to indicate whether you are on the right path as you are taking part in an activity.

This latter part may be the most difficult, and it partly depends on prior experience. Surgeons, in a way, have it easy. Their working environment and activities involve a number of machines which provide feedback regarding a patient's condition. Surgeons can also directly perceive whether or not, for example, there is an exterior bleed. It is somewhat more difficult for a psychiatrist or psychologist conducting sessions with their clients. But even they can tell if their questions are hitting a nerve based on their clients' responses. If, on the other hand, you are learning how to play an instrument, it is of significant importance that you are able to hear the difference between a note that is played on- or off-key, and that you have some inclination as to how the piece you are performing should sound.

There are countless ways to experience flow, such as during work-related activities, sports, games, music, hobbies, dancing, relationships, yoga, martial arts, reading, looking at paintings, and listening to music. The important thing is that you take part in activities that matter to you, that you enjoy, and that challenge you to explore and reinforce your strengths. If you listen to music in order to improve your listening skills and musical knowledge, becoming absorbed in the activity, and experiencing joy, then that is flow. There is no flow in listening to music as a way of filling up the background while you are reading a book, in trying to bone up on your knowledge of classical composers in order to impress your parents-in-law. Music as background noise is not the focus of your attention, and music as a way to impress others is grounded in extrinsic motivation.

Anyone can experience flow, and you do not need to look for it in major challenges or exceptional achievements. You should not expect to experience the entirety of your life in the zone – that is simply not realistic, if even possible. The trick is to start small, for example by taking on a new challenge at work based on your strengths, looking for a sports-based challenge that focuses on the game instead of the outcome, or look for a hobby or leisure activity that gives you such a level of satisfaction that you become skilled at taking part in it step by step. The exercises following this introduction will help you on your way.

Dog (and Master) in the Zone?

Finley is a 3-year-old Toller. He is an inquisitive dog that loves a playful challenge. As soon as he is off the lead, he becomes fully absorbed in his surroundings, following his nose along roads and pathways. Then, his master takes a blue frisbee from his backpack – and Finley's focus narrows instantly. His face looks concentrated, even fierce. As his master prepares to throw the frisbee, Finley quivers in anticipation. They have learnt how to play this game together, Finley and his master. At first, they were pathetic at it. Frisbees that were thrown too high hit Finley on the nose; frisbees that were thrown too low were impossible for him to catch. It is all about timing the throw, connecting with each other, jumping at the right time. They keep getting better and better. When Finley snatches the blue disk from the air, both players rejoice. Finley wags his tail, and his master enthusiastically encourages him to return the frisbee. They are absorbed by the activity, paying no attention to anything else. Their joy is infectious; passers-by stop to encourage the two. Finley and his master hardly notice this; they are intensely involved in their game.

Flow and positive living

Positive living is the ability to experience joy in everyday life. Flow-experiences contribute to this ability in various ways, because these experiences reinforce the basic needs described in Chapter 2: autonomy, experiencing competence, and connectedness to other people and things around you. Fulfilling the basic needs is the most important prerequisite to personal growth.

Flow manifests and develops when you apply your strengths and when you are intrinsically motivated. You take part in an activity because you feel it is important, interesting, and fun, and you are confident in your own abilities. You challenge yourself and are better able to deal with new challenges. The activities you take part in lead to increased enjoyment and energy. While in the flow, you are preoccupied in a less rigid way. Your deeper level of concentration focuses the various 'parts' of your humanity, your thoughts, intentions, emotions, and senses, on the same goal. Afterwards, you will experience a greater sense of unity, both with yourself and with your surroundings and others around you. The connection to your surroundings is strengthened when you share in your flow-experience, or if it is part of an activity shared by others, such as two tennis players testing each other's skills to the limit, or musicians performing together in an orchestra.

Csíkszentmihályi (2001, p. 101) provides a wonderful summary of the contribution of flow to positive living: 'The flow-experience has the capacity to make our lives richer, more intense, and more meaningful'.

Some side-notes

This is where we discuss several important caveats. The flow-experience is often confused with any relaxing activity – this is a mistake. Watching a relaxing TV show or playing a relaxing game may well put you in a state where you forget about yourself, and lose track of time – just as you would during a flow-experience. In that sense, the things are comparable. It is pleasant to forget about your self-preoccupation and your worries as a result of taking part in a relaxing activity. But the difference between a relaxing activity and a flow-inducing activity is that the latter tests and improves the limits of your abilities, thereby causing you to experience personal growth. Taking part in an activity that is merely relaxing, however, leaves you the same person as you were before. Flow-activities leave you more skilful.

But do not forget to keep a sense of perspective. Experiencing flow at all times, under all circumstances, is impossible. No doubt there are people who may come close, but it is an incredibly high standard to set yourself – one that may lead to disappointment. There may be some excellent reasons to choose routine or certainty at certain stages. Some sense of security in your life is, if nothing else, a comforting thought. Some worries you experience may be very real ones, and may lead you to be able to pay less attention to your activities.

Problems arise if your desire for security, for status, or for wealth begins to take control of your life, if you come to rely on these things, or if you become so engrossed with your worries that you can no longer pay any attention to your daily activities. This creates a risk of focusing on perceived threats or future goals at the cost of everyday joy. You risk turning your life into a prison of routine. In time, this will continue to suck the joy from your life at an increasing rate.

We feel that experiencing flow is not so much a matter of forcing you to change part of yourself or to learn new skills. We feel it is more to do with recognizing the limitations that keep you from experiencing flow, and with removing these limitations where possible. Only then should you begin creating the circumstances that open the door to your flow. You could engage in activities which use your strengths, which you are intrinsically motivated to take part in, and which require you to focus on what it is you are doing.

Everyday flow – exercises

The first four exercises deal with general ways of introducing flow into your life. These are followed by a number of exercises about flow-experiences, specifically aimed at working life.

Exercise 1: Changing 'have to' to 'want to'

1. Make a list of all the things that you do not enjoy doing, but that you nevertheless feel you have to do because you do not have any other choice. Once you have finished this list, you will have an overview of all the things you are reluctant to do. Does your list seem short or long? What effects do these activities have on your life? The next step in this exercise can help you view some activities in a different light.

2. Next, establish why you choose to take part in each activity, and what you accomplish by taking part in them. First of all, you should realize that even 'have to' activities are subject to a choice, and that there are often underlying needs or values involved. You can discover what these are by completing the following sentence for each activity: 'I choose to take part in X because it contributes to the need for . . . or because it ties in with my values regarding . . .'. You may discover an underlying positive value or intrinsic motivation for the activities you evaluate. This can help you experience an activity differently.

To illustrate, here is an example of a man who hates having to cut the grass, and views this as a 'have to' activity. His wife tends to remind him that the grass needs clipping, and he feels he only does it because she tells him to. That does not have the makings of intrinsic motivation. By completing the sentence, he uncovers the following underlying value: 'I choose to cut the grass instead of tiling the garden, because I enjoy kicking the ball around with my son.' This is a clearly intrinsic motivation, which can help our protagonist view this chore in a different light. He may still not enjoy doing it, but the underlying value changes the way he perceives the activity.

What do you do with those activities that you find it impossible to link to any form of intrinsic motivation? Drop them altogether? Cut back on them? Someone who does not enjoy cutting the grass may decide to put down tiles instead, or to move to a house that does not have grass once the children are older.

Tip: to do, or not to do?

We are often faced with the dilemma: Should I, or shouldn't I? You may have received a request or offer to do something. One of the most helpful things you can do in this case is not to immediately respond 'Yes' or 'No', but first to consider the matter. That does not have to come at the cost of perceived spontaneity. You can be enthusiastic and let people know, and still ask for a little time to think things through. Take your time to establish your motives. Even if you come up with a plan or idea yourself it is always good to examine your motivations.

Be alert for the following extrinsic motivations:

- Because you are looking for recognition;
- Because you fear being hurt in your pride;
- Because you can earn money even though you actually do not need it;
- Because you do not want to disappoint others;
- Because you simply excel at it; and
- Because you wish to avoid conflict.

Intrinsic motivations would look more like this:

- Because you enjoy doing it;
- Because you want to help someone out (by investing part of yourself);
- Because you feel it ties in with your goals and values; and
- Because you feel it is an exciting challenge of your strengths.

Exercise 2: Flow-experiences

This chapter explained the concept of flow. Flow is felt during the times when you are fully absorbed in an activity, when you are intrinsically motivated because you enjoy the activity itself, or when you feel the purpose of the activity matters to you. The challenge and your skills are in balance, and you are confident that you can achieve your target.

Consider the time or times you (have) experience(d) flow. Describe these experiences. What were you doing? What was the context, and where did it take place? What was your purpose? Were you on your own, or with others? There may be a particular time in your life during which you seemed to continuously experience greater periods of flow. What did a typical day look like during that period?

Exercise 3: How much flow are you experiencing?

This exercise is intended to make you aware of any current limitations that are preventing you from experiencing flow. Consider your life as it is now. Review the past week. Are there times when you experienced flow? Is your life subject to routine? How much? What do your evenings look like? What activities involve challenging yourself, using and developing your strengths and qualities? We are not talking about the times when you feel relaxed. Flow is not concerned with the times you enjoy watching TV, or are having a comfortable chat with a partner, friends, or acquaintances. Relaxation is important, but it is not the topic of this chapter.

If you are having difficulties recalling moments when you experienced flow, try to determine if one of the following issues may be preventing it from reaching you. Try not to judge yourself for encountering resistance. Finding out the things that are inhibiting your flow is a good thing; it provides you with a means to accomplish change.

- What is your motivation for and during the activities you take part in? Do you mainly undertake activities to please others or live up to their expectations? Are you mostly result-oriented?
- Which strengths do your activities address? Are they too focused on using learned behaviours or weaknesses?

Do you experience frustration and stress during most of the activities you take part in?

- Do the challenges tie in with your abilities? Are the challenges in your life too big and/or not appropriate to your strengths? Or are you not challenged enough?
- Are you able to remain focused on the activity? Are you often distracted by your thoughts or worries? Are you mainly focused on the results?
- Do you receive sufficient feedback while taking part in the activity? If you are not (made) aware that you are on the right track, reaching it becomes difficult.

Exercise 4: Introduce flow into your life: challenging activity

Try to find an activity that lends itself to manifesting flow. You may come up with something straight away. You could also have another look at what you discovered during this chapter, that is, what you have come up with so far. What are your strengths? Pick something that ties in with those. Try something that seems worthwhile to you. Not because you hope it will earn you others' appreciation, not because it is functional, not because you hope to reach something with it. The possibilities are endless. Flow can manifest through music, yoga, sports, martial arts, cookery, studies, language, literature, writing, nature, and so on.

Once you have had one or more ideas, take the next couple of days to examine what you have come up with. Find information online, read a book on the subject, talk to people you know are involved in it. What does it entail? What skills does it address? Make note of what you experience. Do you feel inspired? Does your idea that this activity could be used to manifest flow seem justified? Visit a try-out or a class if your idea lends itself to that.

Another way of processing your ideas is through an exercise of imagination. Based on what you know and have learnt, imagine that you are taking part in your chosen activity. Take some time to do so. Pick a quiet moment.

Close your eyes, and takes several deep breaths in and out. Then imagine you are taking part in the activity. What do you experience?

The final step is in execution. Answer the following questions:

- What is your objective?
- How will you obtain feedback? How will you know you are heading in the right direction?
- What steps are you going to take to realize your aim?
- What are your pitfalls? Think of things like: being too quick to give up, or becoming too focused on results.

Flow at work – exercises

The following exercises are concerned with achieving the flow-state in your work. As part of the previous chapter, you thoroughly paid attention to your strengths. When you use a strength, you are able to handle an activity well while becoming energized at the same time. Based on various exercises and possible discussions with colleagues, friends and loved ones, you have come up with an overview of several of your strengths. You have differentiated between strengths and learned behaviours. Learned behaviours may also be things you excel at, but mastering them took effort, and they do not make you feel energized.

The goal now is to create a more challenging work environment. This should be done based on your strengths, potentially leading you to increasingly experience flow. There is a lot to be gained in allowing your unrealized strengths to come to the surface, and thereby expressing them.

Exercise 5: Flow-experiences at work

Can you identify moments of flow in your work? Moments where you were completely absorbed by what you were doing; challenged but capable; confident you could reach your target, a target you felt mattered. Write down a list of these moments of flow. Take some time during the course of the week to describe your experiences. What were you doing? What was the context? Where were you? What was your intended goal? Where you alone, or with others? What did you experience?

There may be a particular time at work during which you seemed to continuously experience greater periods of flow. What did a typical day during that period look like?

Exercise 6: Your motivation

Read through what you have written down so far. What inspires you in your work? Why did you take it up? What are you passionate about? Why do you do what you do? What are your most important work-needs? Formulate the intrinsic motivation you had for your work, since these are the handholds for enjoying it. It is also possible that you will find that your motivation was mainly extrinsic. Say, for example, that you chose this work for your parents' recognition, to impress your peers, to earn money, to improve your status. In that case, this exercise may be confronting, since extrinsic motivation does not provide any handholds for enjoyment. You may have found some sort of satisfaction in your work over time, and your motivation may have shifted to a more intrinsic form; but you may come to the conclusion that your work does not (entirely) suit you. If that is the case, thinking about your motivation may feel confrontational.

Exercise 7: Task and strength analysis

a. What are your assigned tasks at work? What percentage of your time is spent on these tasks? Which strengths can you apply to each task?

Table 3.1 Analysis

Task	% of time/week	Applied/applicable strength

b. Which tasks would you like to expand upon because they are a good match for your strengths and tie in with your motivation and needs?

c. Which new task would you like to take up based on your strengths?

d. Which strength could you make more/better use of in your work?

e. What can you do to further develop the strengths used for important tasks? What do you wish to excel at? Do you have a strength that is still resting below the surface, a strength you could make better use of and develop further? As indicated, the greatest opportunity for personal growth and job satisfaction is found in the realm of untapped strengths.

f. What important problem(s) are you currently facing at work? Which strength could help you solve or deal with it?

Exercise 8: Learned behaviours and weaknesses

Exercise 1 on page 32 involved defining some of your learned behaviours. These are things you have come to be good at, but which do not make you feel joyful or energized. Write down your learned behaviours once more. Then, write down your weaknesses. What is it that you are not good at, and what can you only improve through gargantuan effort?

The following questions are aimed at teaching you to moderate the use of your learned behaviours, and to minimize the number of confrontations with your weaknesses. For each learned behaviour and weakness, answer the following questions:

a. Can you give it up? In some situations, using the learned behaviours may have become force of habit – all things considered, you may not find using them a hardship. Your colleagues will not be able to distinguish between strengths and learned behaviours; you are the only one who knows whether or not you are enjoying yourself. You colleagues will automatically approach you with tasks that require the use of your learned behaviours. But these are the activities that will cause you to burn out in the long run, because they do not provide energy.

b. Can you provide a different structure or focus to the tasks you are performing? A reorganization may allow you to reduce the frequency with which you have to apply your learned behaviours or weaknesses. Can you use your strengths to compensate for your weakness?

c. Is it possible to organize your activities into 'skill sandwiches'? This means alternating between energizing and required, non-energizing activities that may not appeal to your strengths.

d. Is there a colleague who complements your skillset? Someone whose strengths make up for your learned behaviours or weaknesses, and vice versa.

e. Consider whether it may be possible to organize your team based on strengths. Implementing this type or reorganization requires cooperation from your superior(s) and colleagues. Most organizations think in terms of tasks, whereas structuring according to employee strength can also be a valid premise. What are each employee's strengths, and how can these be applied to meet team targets?

f. In case you are still required to perform tasks that put you face to face with your weaknesses: Is it possible to follow some sort of training course designed to help you reach 'acceptable' levels? By limiting your investment in such tasks, you will retain energy which you can use to further develop your strengths.

Exercise 9: Formulate concrete goals and actions

The previous exercises provided you with insight into the possibility of:

- Making better use of your strengths and developing them in your work;
- Moderating the application of your learned behaviours; and
- Minimizing the application of your weaknesses.

You can now translate these possibilities into concrete goals and actions. Select at least one action aimed at further developing or better using a strength at work. The goal is that, in time, you will come to find that your strengths and your work complement each other better, and that you will take more enjoyment and gain more energy from your work.

The following action plan form can be used to flesh out your goals and actions. We have provided an example in the form of Bert's goal and action plan. Bert found that creativity is one of his strengths, but that he hardly makes use of this strength in his work. He works in admin, and his performance has been satisfactory year in, year out. He has been using his learned behaviours throughout his career, which has become a massive drain on his resources in recent years. His employer is willing to help Bert investigate the possibility of changing Bert's work activities to increase his enjoyment in his work. In his spare time, Bert spends a lot of time on social media, and on designing apps. Then, one day, at lunch, Bert learns that the company is intending to recruit an external agency to create a new website.

Table 3.2 Bert's goal and action plan

What is your main goal?	To make more use of my creative strengths at work to improve my energy level
What intermediate goal do you wish to achieve in four weeks' time? This goal should be *concrete* and *measurable*.	• A talk with my employer regarding my wish to be substantially involved in the development of our new website. • Writing down ideas about our company's social media profile; come up with an app which people can use to review their administration.
What actions will you need to take for the next two to four weeks? Are these actions realistic? Can these actions be executed? Are these actions concrete?	• Set up a meeting with my employer. • Fleshing out ideas on paper. Yes Yes Yes
What are you going to do *where*, *when* and with *whom*?	• I will being writing down ideas tonight. • The meeting with my employer is scheduled for next week.
Which of your strengths can you apply to achieve your goal?	Creativity, decisiveness, efficiency, drive, eye for improvement, relationship-based skills.
How can you remind yourself of your required actions?	I don't need to, I look forward to them.

Table 3.3 Goal and action plan

What is your main goal?	
What intermediate goal do you wish to achieve in four weeks' time? This goal should be *concrete* and *measurable*.	
What actions will you need to take for the next two to four weeks? Are these actions realistic? Can these actions be executed? Are these actions concrete?	
What are you going to do *where*, *when* and with *whom*?	
Which of your strengths can you apply to achieve your goal?	
How can you remind yourself of your required actions?	

Tips and considerations

You are recommended to develop your plans in consultation with your supervisor and colleagues in order to arrive at an improved match between your strengths and job tasks. Changes to your job description, of course, require your supervisor's consent. Any managers aware that this will lead to increased motivation and job satisfaction will hopefully agree to work with you on achieving this: Ensuring employees are motivated is in their best interests. It is best to be honest about why you want to pursue this goal, and what it would mean for the organization. If it should prove impossible to consult on job adjustments, then look for other areas in your work where you have room to improve the conditions to your benefit. You may be able to reallocate time from other projects.

An important question you should answer for yourself is whether your work motivation corresponds to the organization's vision. If it does, finding a match between your strengths and your job tends to become much easier. If it does not, that may complicate matters. It is possible that you may conclude that you had better look for employment elsewhere.

You should realize that there are always tasks that do not correspond to your strengths or motivation, but that are nevertheless part of your job description because they are important to the organization. You may experience these more in terms of 'have to' than 'want to'. It is possible to become mired in your resistance to and complaints against these tasks, and also risk having them influence your enjoyment of other tasks. The previous exercise already provided you with other possibilities for dealing with your weaknesses. And when dealing with a task you do not feel motivated to do, consider the following possibilities:

- Perform these tasks with others at specific times. Try to make it a fun, communal affair, and maybe hang out together afterwards.
- Teach yourself to perform these tasks as efficiently as possible. Challenge yourself into reaching maximum results using minimum effort!

If you come to find that your motivation does not conform to the organization's vision (any more), and if you cannot find new challenges or flow in your work, you may decide that it is time to move on to a different job. That may be much easier said than done. If finding a new job in the short term proves impossible, then try to apply your strengths during your spare time, to find the flow and the challenges that way. Alternatively, it may be possible to reduce your hours, providing you with more time to learn new skills or take part in challenging courses that can help you to find work that ties in with your needs and passion in the long term.

References

Csíkszentmihályi, M. (2001). *Flow: Psychologie van de optimale ervaring. (Flow: Psychology of optimal experience)*. Amsterdam: Boom uitgevers Amsterdam.

Rosenberg, M.B. (2015). *Nonviolent communication: A language of life*. Encinitas CA: Puddledancer Press.

Chapter 4

Optimists are full of it!

Introduction

Never stop learning, never stop developing yourself; these are two important conditions to experiencing well-being. Whatever projects you undertake, be they large or small, they should matter to you, and give meaning to your life. You are heading in a certain direction, towards an intended future; a future that you feel is worthwhile, worth working hard to achieve, worth applying your strengths to. Achieving your desired goals is a matter of trial and error. Successes are irrevocably alternated with obstacles in your path. Not every first try will be a success, and you will deal with adversity. And when you do, you will need your faith in the future. Be confident in your abilities to shape your life the way you want to. Positive psychology, therefore, pays a lot of attention to optimism and hope. Optimism and hope are both traits you can teach yourself. This chapter discusses optimism and hope in greater detail, and provides you with exercises you can use to strengthen these feelings.

Optimism and hope

Learned helplessness

Research into optimism is closely linked with Martin Seligman, one of the founders of positive psychology. In 1990, he wrote a book on optimism titled *Learned optimism: How to change your mind and your life*. Seligman initially conducted a lot of research into the causes of depression. One of the characteristics of depression is the absence of faith in the future. Seligman found that, among other things, this had to do with acquiring hopelessness. He devised the following experiment and divided his subjects into three groups. The first group was confronted with a disruptive but non-damaging event: a sudden loud noise. When these people pressed a button, the noise would stop immediately. In other words, these people were in control of events. The second group was confronted with the same loud noise. They did not have the possibility of making the noise stop; they could only endure the racket, which was turned on or off without their intervention. The third group was faced with nothing; no button, no sound. Sometime later, the participants took part in the second part of the experiment. All participants placed their hand inside a box. If they moved their hand to the left side of the box, a loud noise would sound; if they moved their hand to the right, the noise would turn off. As it turns out, people in the first and third groups were quick to move their hand around the box to the right side, thereby turning off the noise. But the people in the second group remained passive. They did nothing, and suffered through the noise if they placed their hand in the left side of the box. They acted helplessly. And this helplessness was an acquired frame of mind, resulting from their time spent in an unpleasant situation beyond their control. Follow-up studies showed that this learned helplessness transferred across different situations. You can imagine that this helplessness was a source of listlessness and sadness.

Optimist v. pessimist interpretations

Seligman and his colleagues also discovered something else. Around a third of the test subjects in the group that had no control over the noise proved immune to the induced feeling of helplessness. During the second part of the experiment as well as during other situations, they actively kept trying to find ways of making an unpleasant situation stop. Other subjects appeared helpless before the experiment was even fully underway. What was causing this divide? Seligman looked for an explanation by examining people's feelings concerning the unpleasant situation: their interpretation of what was happening. He divided the subjects into two groups: optimists and pessimists.

The optimists had a remarkably different interpretation of the situation compared to the pessimists. Whenever optimists experienced something unpleasant, their thoughts on the situation looked something like this: It is *temporary*, *external* and *specific* (born from particular circumstances). If they were to fail an exam, they might say: 'I was unable to properly focus because I did not sleep well.' Which is actually a way of saying: I can probably do better next time. Incidentally, this group indicated that success was always a result of their own efforts. The pessimists looked at the situation very differently. Their explanation for negative events was expressed in terms of thoughts like: *permanent*, *internal*, and *universal*. They might look at the same failed exam and say: 'I did not understand the questions; it was too difficult for me.' In other words: The problem is my lack of intelligence, which is insurmountable. This group of people was more prone to assigning success to the influence of external circumstances. It is all a matter of interpretation. People with an optimist mind-set do not get helpless; people with a pessimist mind-set always act helpless.

In summary, the more people are pessimistic, the more they ascribe negative events to their own, permanent weaknesses, and positive events to circumstances. The more people are optimistic, the more they ascribe negative events to temporary circumstances, and positive events to their strengths.

Hope

In addition to Seligman's research, a second notion of optimism was developed; one that better ties in with goal-based operating. Based on their studies, psychologists Carver and Scheier (2002) concluded that people organize their life and behaviour using attainable and desired goals. They defined optimism as the general expectation that the future will hold more positive and desired outcomes than negative or unwanted ones. People with a generally positive outlook more often think they will be able to reach their goals, and will persevere in their efforts longer than people with a more negative outlook. People with a generally positive outlook expect things to turn out to their advantage, that they will always turn out fine, and that they will experience more good things than bad.

The idea of the future being better than the current situation is called 'hope'. In his compelling book *Man's search for meaning*, Viktor Frankl describes the connection between hope and the survival chances of fellow prisoners in a concentration camp (see the text on page 112). He writes: '. . . any attempt to restore a man's inner strength in the camp had first to succeed in showing him some future goal' (1978, p. 98).

Scientist Shane Lopez investigates the relationship between hope and well-being. People who are already hopeful that a future goal can be reached experience a greater sense of well-being, and also stand a greater chance of achieving a desired goal. He describes research (Snyder et al., 2010) which indicated that people who are hopeful are better able to deal with physical pain. He describes hope as an activating impulse, one that drives us to act in order to achieve a desired goal. He states that hope comprises four core aspects, being: 1) The idea that the future will be better than the now; 2) The conviction that one is able to influence the future while being aware of one's own limits; 3) An understanding that there is more than one way to reach a goal, and lastly, that 4) No path is without its obstacles.

Hope is not the same as wishing for a better future. Wishing does not involve taking action; wishing implies that you are not going to take action to achieve your goal. Popular psychology long held the idea that, as long as you keep a positive mind-set, good things will happen to you. That often leads to disappointment, because positive thoughts did not lead to the desired result – in fact, it can promote a passive, victimized role. You obviously need an extra something, such as recognizing the moment, and value-driven action. Recognizing the moment means not resisting that which is there now. This was covered extensively in the book *A beginner's guide to mindfulness: Live in the moment*. Recognition means not throwing in the towel but taking value-driven action to help you achieve your goals. Value-driven action is action based on what you feel is truly important. It is possible to learn new skills and develop new qualities as you go, which will increase your possibilities of achieving your goals.

Both Frankl and Lopez point out that it is not the past or the present that is the largest determining factor for the future; it is the will to be meaningful, and the hope to realize this future.

The birth of optimism

Optimism is partly genetic, but only for around 25 per cent. The means that some people naturally have a more positive view of the future than others. Optimism is also developed during childhood, and is the result of parents' or guardians' reactions to a child's experience of success or failure. If parents or guardians pay more attention to a child's own input in cases of success, and more attention to the role of circumstances in cases of failure, the child's optimism is reinforced. This is in contrast to developing pessimism, where the emphasis is placed on one's own input in case of failure, and on circumstances in case of success.

In addition, families that are subject to greater levels of tension, for example, as a result of financial concerns, relationship problems, or lack of attention to children, may exhibit increased pessimism. The fact that optimism or pessimism can be taught would indicate that change is possible. Studies confirm this, because an optimist attitude can be taught. This assumes that the optimist or pessimist interpretation of an event is dictated by behavioural patterns which we can be made aware of, thus allowing us to adjust them. Studies also show that it is possible to teach yourself a more positive outlook, assuring you that you can reach your goals.

Optimism's effects on your health

There has been a lot of research into the effects of optimism. Part of that research has focused on the effects of optimism on physical health. In general, people who are more optimistic are found to have smaller risks of certain physical conditions, such as heart conditions. They are also found to recuperate from illness more quickly, and chronic diseases in optimistic people do not seem to deteriorate as quickly (Peters et al., 2013).

Major research in the US (Tindle et al., 2009) followed nearly a hundred thousand middle-aged women over the course of eight years. They were frequently asked to fill in various questionnaires, including one designed to measure optimism. Researchers also kept track of whether any members of the group passed away during those eight years, and what the causes of any deaths had been. This investigation showed that people who were very optimistic had a 14 per cent lower chance of dying that people who were not optimistic. During the eight years the group was monitored, the risk of death from cardiovascular diseases among very optimistic group members was in fact 30 per cent lower. Peters et al. (2013) also discuss other studies which indicate that optimism has an effect on life expectancy. Another part of the investigation looked into the relationship between optimism and physical health. It intensively followed students, employees, and elderly men, and others, over the course of many years. Participants in these investigations whose outlook was more optimistic still had lower chances of having depression-related complaints for many years after.

Optimism does have an effect on our physical and mental health, as well as our life expectancy. On top of that, optimism contributes to your ability to lead an enjoyable and meaningful life.

Reinforcing optimism and hope – exercises

Exercise 1: Be kinder to yourself

This exercise was originally conceived by Martin Seligman (1990). Using this exercise, you will become aware of your interpretations of negative events or adversity, and teach you to challenge your negative interpretations. This exercise consists of three steps:

Step 1: Keep an ABC diary

A is for 'adversity': the occurrence of negative events or setbacks.
For A, describe the negative event; be as concrete as possible. What actually happened? Do not describe feelings or emotions. Negative events you cover may be both minor and major ones.

B is for 'beliefs': the interpretations and convictions you hold about the event.
For B, describe your thoughts about the event. Do not describe your feelings yet.

C is for 'consequences': the feelings and behaviour that resulted from your beliefs.
For C, describe your feelings and concrete actions following the event.

Here are two examples:

Table 4.1 Example: Eric

A(dversity)
I booked a trip at a travel organisation, transferred the money, but the agency turns out not to exist. I have been conned. Notifying the police will not help me get my money back.
B(eliefs)
'It is not right', 'This should not happen to me', 'These people should be punished', 'I am naive.'
C(onsequences)
Feeling: anger, shame
Behaviour: looking for information about the culprit only, reading about fellow victims' experiences, reading about applicable legislation, finding comfort in the idea that this can also happen to others.

Table 4.2 Example: Irene

A(dversity)
A friend does not return my calls.
B(eliefs)
'She thinks I do not matter', 'I am not interesting.'
C(onsequences)
Feeling: sadness
Behaviour: I turn inward, and cancel a meeting with another friend.

Do this for three to five negative events over the course of several days.

Table 4.3 An ABC diary

A(dversity)
B(eliefs)
C(onsequences)

A(dversity)
B(eliefs)
C(onsequences)

A(dversity)
B(eliefs)
C(onsequences)

A(dversity)
B(eliefs)
C(onsequences)

A(dversity)
B(eliefs)
C(onsequences)

Step 2: Review what you wrote down

- Do you recognize certain patterns? What are your 'favourite' pessimist thoughts?
- How have you interpreted the event? Do you tend to find their causes with yourself? Do you think every negative event is evidence of your immutable personal negative characteristics?
- What is the result of the pessimist statements, for example sadness or passivity?

Eric notes that his anger is realistic, because he has been conned. He thinks most people in his position would be angry. He does know that he has a tendency to go overboard where his sense of justice is concerned. He cannot accept that people who profit from duping others. Now that he has written everything down, he is surprised to feel ashamed. He nevertheless does recognize a pattern of placing the blame with himself.

Irene recognizes the pessimist pattern immediately. She is quick to feel rejected, curl up in a corner, and become passive. The sadness she feels is familiar.

Step 3: Dismantle your pessimist thoughts

Employ either of the following two methods, using whatever method you find appealing or familiar.

Method 1: Challenging your thoughts

This method is frequently used in cognitive behavioural therapy. Challenging your thoughts is about examining to what extent your thoughts are realistic, whether there are other interpretations possible, and whether these thoughts are helping you along. The latter part means that, while some thoughts may be correct, the consequences of repeating them may have very negative effects, especially for you yourself.

Examining the reality of your thoughts can be done by asking yourself what proof you have that your thoughts are correct, and whether there are no alternative explanations possible. You will find that many of your thoughts are not based on truth. You may wonder why your thoughts are shaped a certain way. The explanation for this is in earlier experiences and conditioning. Once you realize your thoughts do not describe reality, what happens to your mood and behaviour?

Eric feels that his thoughts 'It is not fair' and 'These people should be punished' are correct. At the same time, he knows he can go overboard, especially in continuing to look for information about the individuals, relevant legislation, and similar experiences. Searching for this information seems to fuel his anger rather than quell it.

The thought 'This should not happen to me' is factually incorrect, since injustice is a very real thing, and it really did happen to him. Eric realizes he needs to come to terms with this. He now knows that his thought 'I am naive' is incorrect. When Eric notified the police, he was told that the word 'artist' in 'con-artist' is not accidental. Many people fall victim to these tricks. Eric knows this experience means he is unlikely to fall for the same trick again.

Eric formulates an alternative thought: 'There is injustice in the world. I have been made a victim of it, but I have done what I could and I have learned from it.' This new interpretation allows him more room to breathe.

Irene's past negative experiences have made her prone to feeling rejected, making her feel insecure. The friend who did not return the call had been ill that week, and Irene's thought 'She thinks I do not matter' was most definitely not correct. Now that she knows this, Irene realizes how quickly she falls for these types of pessimist thoughts. She also realizes that her thought 'I do not matter' follows the pessimist thoughts directly, leading to a subsequent sad mood and passive attitude.

Irene formulates an alternative thought: 'My friend was ill and therefore did not return my call' and 'If someone does not return my call, then that may not be related to me at all.'

Method 2: Defusing your thoughts

If you are familiar with mindfulness *acceptance and commitment therapy*, and have read the book *A beginner's guide to mindfulness: Live in the moment* for example, you can also defuse your pessimist thoughts. This means moving away from your thoughts because you know that they do not reflect reality. Your mind is a factory of thoughts and stories, and it is possible that your mind tends toward pessimist products.

Thoughts are mental events that come and go. Recognize your mind's favoured thoughts and stories, notice them, and let them slowly fade into the background. Or choose a method that helps you to do so, for example, by articulating them using the phrase 'I am having a thought that says . . .', or give names to your most frequent thoughts and stories. Or do the mindfulness exercise from *A beginner's guide to mindfulness: Live in the moment* (Bohlmeijer and Hulsbergen, 2013, pp. 114–115) where you observe your thoughts and notice the process of thinking.

Irene chooses this method because, though she understands her thoughts are not correct, they are nevertheless frequently on her mind. Challenging them does not lead to a decrease in their prevalence. These are thoughts that are not worth the effort, thoughts that make her feel insecure. As soon as she notices these types of thoughts in her mind, she greets them: 'Hello Insecurity, welcome.' Naming her thoughts helps her to stay afloat instead of sinking into a pessimist thought stream, to avoid lapsing into negative behaviour.

Exercise 2: Visualise your best possible self

This exercise was developed and researched by Madelon Peters and her colleagues at Maastricht University (2013). It helps you face the future with full confidence.

Read the following instructions first before doing the exercise. Choose a quiet time of day, and a quiet room where you will not be interrupted. Sit down, get comfortable, and close your eyes. Using this exercise, you are going to visualize yourself in the future. You have worked hard to develop yourself. You have succeeded in achieving all of your life goals. You can think of this as the moment when all of your life's dreams have come true, and you have optimized all of your capabilities.

- What is your future life like?
- What are your most important characteristics?
- Which strengths have you developed, and how do you apply them?
- What worthwhile feats have you performed?
- What long-cherished goals and desires have you realized?

Consider the following domains:

- The personal domain: personal characteristics, strengths, as well as what you look like at that point in your life.
- The relational domain: What are your most important relationships like? How can they be characterized? What is taking place?
- The professional domain: What position do you hold? What professional achievements have your performed? What is it like to apply your expertise and experience flow? How do you contribute to society?

Take your time for each domain, thereby visualizing your ideal future. Then, write down on paper what you visualize in each domain. Do not be concerned with writing a coherent story. Write down what comes to you, what you perceive. Do try to be as concrete as possible.

Try to do this visualization exercise for five minutes every day for the coming week (just the visualization, no writing). Choose a single domain every day. Schedule your visualization sessions to take place at the same time every day. Make it a routine. Look at these times as moments of inspiration that you create for yourself, moments that will help you lead a positive life.

Exercise 3: Imagine the near future

Exercise 2 was used to apply your imagination to visualizing your optimum capabilities and your best possible self. Research (Meevissen et al., 2011) shows that this exercise, if done every day for at least two weeks, actually increases your optimism, thereby contributing to your development and the achieving of your life goals. When you feel that this exercise is having a positive effect, you can also use your imagination to help you realize your short-term goals. This is done as follows.

As part of Chapter 3, you considered goals and actions to help you develop and make more use of your strengths. That does not happen overnight. In order to achieve a goal, you will often need to take several intermediate steps. Every time you schedule an action, you can use your imagination. Imagine you are performing the action. Visualize exactly what could happen. If you required input from others, visualize their different possible reactions, and your response to their reactions born from your strong desire to realize something. Do this at least three times before actually performing the action. This improves your chances of success.

References

Bohlmeijer, E.T., and Hulsbergen, M.L. (2013). *A beginner's guide to mindfulness: Live in the moment.* London: McGraw-Hill.

Carver, C., and Scheier, M. (2002). Optimism. In: C. Snyder and S. Lopez (Eds.), *Handbook of Positive Psychology.* New York: Oxford University Press.

Frankl, V. (1978). *De zin van het bestaan. (Meaning of life).* Rotterdam: Ad Donker bv.

Meevissen, Y.M.C., Peters, M.L., and Alberts, H.J.E.M. (2011). Become more optimistic by imagining a best possible self: Effects of a two week intervention. *Journal of Behavior Therapy and Experimental Psychiatry, 42,* 371–378.

Peters, M.L. Rius Ottenheim, N., and Giltay, E. (2013). Optimisme (Optimism). In: E.T. Bohlmeijer, L. Bolier, G.J. Westerhof, and J.A. Walburg (eds), *Handboek Positieve psychologie, theorie, onderzoek en toepassingen. (Handbook of Positive Psychology: theory, research and applications)*. Amsterdam: Boom uitgevers Amsterdam.

Seligman, M. (1990). *Learned optimism: How to change your mind and your life*. New York: Knopf.

Snyder, C.R., Lopez, S.J., and Pedrotti, J.T. (2010). *Positive psychology: The scientific and practical exploration of human strengths*. Thousand Oaks CA: Sage Publications.

Chapter 5

Have a break

Introduction

We are often unkind to ourselves; we are more used to judging ourselves critically – our achievements, our looks, our social skills, etc. Our core message to ourselves is that we are not good enough unless we absolutely excel in these areas. There are very few people who will wholeheartedly tell themselves: 'I am satisfied with myself just as I am.' We are also dismissive of ourselves when we become ill, are in pain, or changing physically as a result of becoming older.

In recent years, a lot of research has been conducted that indicates that this critical attitude contributes to feelings of stress, insecurity, aggression, and sadness. It is abundantly clear that a self-critical attitude does not contribute to happiness and well-being. The number one way of becoming unhappy is to focus on the things you are unhappy or unsatisfied with. Positive psychology regards compassion and self-appreciation as important factors contributing to well-being.

This chapter introduces the concepts of compassion and appreciation, and teaches you to develop these qualities. The word 'compassion' is occasionally met with resistance. It sounds soft; it makes people feel weak. This is because of their conviction that you need to be tough in order to remain standing in our society, or that you need to be critical of yourself in order to achieve something. Research shows that this is not the case. Compassion is all about the courage to take wise action to relieve suffering and promote well-being and suffering (Gilbert and Choden, 2013). A compassionate and appreciative attitude towards yourself and others will let you achieve more, and will let you experience greater relaxation and balance. This chapter focuses specifically on self-compassion and self-appreciation. Chapter 8, on connecting, covers compassion for others.

Self-compassion and self-appreciation

The developed brain: benefits and burdens

In order to explain self-compassion, we will first explain a little about the way our brains work. Our brain can be viewed as a layered construction: the brainstem, the limbic system, and the neocortex (Gilbert, 2009). These layers are all connected and function coherently. The brainstem regulates the autonomous nervous system based on reflexes. The limbic system regulates emotions. The neocortex is the upper layer and enables us to think and reflect. Higher species of animal (humans, apes) are different from lower species for several reasons, including their capacity for reflection and thought. Lower species lack this capacity, living and surviving on the basis of their reflexes (autonomous nervous system, brainstem) and emotions (limbic system) instead. The brainstem and limbic system are active in human brains as well. For example, during threatening situations, both amygdalae (the two almond-shaped cores just above the ears) are triggered. Unfortunately, however, these amygdalae do not 'recognize' the difference between real and imaginary threats.

We owe much to our neocortex. Our capacity for thought, our ability to imagine something, to schedule, to consult, to use language, to organize, and to reflect has served us well. It allowed us to develop technology which reduced our dependence on Mother Nature's whims, ensuring we survived as a species. But our capabilities come with a downside, which is that we are able, for example, to imagine all sorts of future threats. Thoughts about possible threats trigger the amygdalae and bring us into a state of readiness, even when there is no real current danger. Self-criticism is one of the abilities a developed brain has, since it allows us to imagine an 'ideal self' which we then compare to our 'current self'. Many people experience a difference between their ideal and current selves. This feeling of inadequacy is experienced as a threat which triggers the amygdalae, the fight or flight response we are subject to at any moment of impending threat. We set to work to better ourselves, driven by fear – even though fear is no basis for learning new skills. In fact, it undermines our efforts.

The neocortex (more specifically the left prefrontal section) also houses our ability to experience compassion and love. Giving or receiving compassion and love are abilities we have all been provided with, since they are traits we are born with – hardwired into the structure of our brains. Research shows that applying these abilities take us to a state of peace, reducing emotions like fear or aggression. Where self-criticism is a form of attacking the self, compassion is a form of nursing it. Brain research shows that activity in the left prefrontal cortex coincides with reduced activity in the limbic system. In other words: compassion and love reduce fear and aggression.

Interestingly, compassion and love in this respect work differently than, for example, relaxation or happiness. We know that fear cannot coexist with relaxation or happiness. People are never simultaneously fearful and relaxed, or fearful and happy. This is different for experiencing compassion, because compassion can coexist with unpleasant emotions like fear, anger, or sadness. Compassion and love are states of feeling that are all-encompassing. The next chapter, on post-traumatic growth, will cover this feature of compassion again, because compassion reinforces the ability to self-heal when processing unpleasant experiences.

The importance of soothing

Psychologist Paul Gilbert (2009) describes human beings as the result of evolutionary developments. Gilbert's vision of our species is apologetic: We did not choose to be born into this body, with this layered brain structure, As such, we cannot be blamed for the problems arising as a result of its complexity. The right insights, attention, and training can enable us to improve the interplay between the parts of our brain, in order to improve our sense of well-being. Whereas the demands and standards we currently impose on ourselves are high, whereas we are critical of ourselves, and whereas we are afraid of possible threats, it is possible to train ourselves to experience greater compassion and love. This requires practise, because it is a biological given that our attention is more easily held by potential threats than positive experiences. This is not a conscious effort, because our species' past survival required us to be on high alert. But the brain is capable of making new connections if its focus is shifted toward enjoyment, compassion, and connectedness.

Gilbert says the first step to compassion for oneself is to be understanding of the circumstances we did not choose to be in. Each of us was put on this earth with complex brain structures, in a fragile body, with our own sexuality, into a particular culture, into a particular time, into a particular family with parents or guardians with their own possibilities or limitations, with genetically determined talents or imperfections. Understanding this allows us to feel responsible for those circumstances we do have a hand in deciding.

Gilbert (in Gilbert and Choden, 2013) defines compassion as the ability to be sensitive and engage with suffering and the courage to take action to alleviate or prevent suffering. The ability to engage with suffering is the first psychology of compassion. It comprises attributes such as care-focused motivation, being sensitive with open attention, empathy and compassionate non-judgement. The skills to actually alleviate suffering are the second psychology of compassion. Examples of these skills are the ability to apply compassionate thinking, to use compassionate imagery and compassionate behaviour.

In order to train ourselves to be more compassionate towards ourselves, it helps to understand how we respond to life's challenges from our neurobiology. Gilbert (2009) describes how, globally speaking, we have three emotion-regulation systems. These are things we have in common with all mammals, being: a threat system, a drive system, and a soothing or affiliation system (see below). In animals, these systems are generally in balance: If there are no threats, if there is no hunger, and if reproduction is assured, then the animal can relax and recover. For the survival of the species, it is important that each system can be activated as soon as it is needed. In humans, however, the three emotion-regulation systems are often out of whack.

The imbalance in humans is born from an under-developed calming system, among other things. Compared to animals, we are not very good at recovering and calming down even if we are safe and our basic needs have been met. In addition, in many people either or both of the other systems are overdeveloped. Some people have a highly developed threat system, always on guard and focused on potential threats, even steeling themselves using aggression. Others are mainly oriented towards finding more resources by chasing and striving for material wealth, status, or power.

THREE EMOTION-REGULATION SYSTEMS (BASED ON GILBERT, 2009)

1. I am always on guard

In order to be able to quickly identify a threat, the threat system is important. Once a threat is identified, the emotions fear, aggression, or disgust are triggered, enabling a human or an animal to act accordingly, for example, by fighting, fleeing, or freezing. Without this system, no species would survive. Once the threat is passed, the system relaxes. Even though the emotions it triggers are unpleasant, they are designed to protect us. This system is always on high-alert, and has been designed to overestimate potential danger – just to be safe. The brain always prioritizes the activation of this system if a threat is perceived, even though it may coincide with something pleasant.

In humans, this system is activated in times of real, imaginary, or supposed danger, but also when we are faced with the fear of being hurt, out of control, or excluded. The brain does not recognize the difference between these diverse kinds of fear, and just goes through the motions of its standard danger response. In some people, this system may be overdeveloped – possibly as a result of traumatic experiences or increased threats during their life (for example, because of little basic family security due to conflicts, being bullied at school, etc.). This system will have had extensive training, and will need only a relatively minor trigger, such as a fearful thought, to activate.

2. I am never satisfied and always want more

The drive system is important to survive and grow. Wants and desires are its motivations, and fulfilling these feelings is pleasant. Without the desire for food, animals would not hunt – and thus they would starve. Without the desire to create offspring, animals would not mate – and thus they would die out. In animals, this system relaxes when the needs are met and there are sufficient resources to ensure survival.

In humans, the drive system can also be activated even if the basic needs have long since been met. This is a good thing, because if we did not have this motivator to propel us forward, we would likely not have gotten past the Stone Age! The system is exhaustively trained in our consumer society, and is handily exploited by commerce. Desires or needs can make us look for more money, more sex, more recognition, more social contacts, more food, more power, more everything. These desires can be satiated only briefly, and can cause a form of agitated drive which can become unpleasant; nothing is ever enough. The basis for this system's continued activation can be found in our childhood, for example, if our parents or guardians loved us only conditionally, such as only if we did well at school. Even though our brain is designed to look for resources and satisfy our wants, the trick in our current society is instead to make conscious choice from the superfluity of available options.

3. I relax and recover

The soothing or affiliation system is important for relaxation and recovery. The feelings are pleasant, but of a different quality to those of the previous system. These feelings include satisfaction, inner peace, and well-being. The hormones endorphin and oxytocin are released, reducing the concentration of the stress hormones cortisol and adrenaline. Without this system, we risk exhaustion. Once this system takes to the foreground, we are able to connect, to be creative, to play. Apart from short-term recovery, this system creates resources or 'reserves' which can be addressed in the long term.

In many of us, this system is insufficiently developed or active. If people have felt little love or appreciation during their lives, then this system will be less developed. In addition, there is little room for this system in our competitive consumer society. Being busy, experiencing stress are things that our society places too much value in. The 'good news' is that this system is not fixed in our brains, and can be activated by giving ourselves the care and love we need, and to enjoy what exists in the moment. Our ability to generate images and thoughts influences the brain, making it easy to activate the defensive systems. The same ability can be used to address the calming system instead. This way, we use the abilities bestowed on us by our neocortex to improve our own well-being. Compassion training aims to activate the calming system, allowing us to restore the balance between the three systems.

The three emotion regulation systems influence the way the autonomous nervous system functions. The nervous system regulates a large number of our bodily functions without us being consciously aware of this; functions like respiration, digestion, blood pressure, heartbeat. Within the autonomous nervous system, activity is alternately shared between the sympathetic and parasympathetic nervous systems. The sympathetic nervous system ensures that the body obtains the energy it needs to take action: The (stress) hormones adrenaline and cortisol are released into our bloodstream, our heart rate quickens, our blood pressure increases, and the digestion decreases. The parasympathetic nervous system influences the organs in a way that allows the body to recover, and activates the digestive system.

The threat system and the drive system lead to the activation of the sympathetic nervous system, while the calming system leads to the activation of the parasympathetic nervous system. The activation of the parasympathetic nervous system involves the hormone oxytocin; this ensures feelings of relaxation, calmness, healing, pain reduction, and connectedness. This hormone, also known as the 'bliss hormone', enables a new-born to bond with its mother through, among other things, touch. Oxytocin is mainly produced as a result of nerves on the skin obtaining information about the outside world, but we are also able to trigger the production of this hormone ourselves (through touch, among other things), through caring and being compassionate to ourselves.

An underdeveloped calming system causes the sympathetic nervous system to go into overdrive, with damaging results to our health (in the long term). For our physical health, the development of a system that calms and relaxes us is of major value. Developing compassion is an important key factor in this process, because it enhances the calming system and reduces the intensity with which we experience emotions. If, in addition to that, we are able appreciate ourselves, we experience increased feelings of satisfaction, allowing us to recuperate and relax.

Self-compassion

In addition to the aforementioned physiological effects, research shows that compassion contributes to well-being and happiness. Psychologist Kristin Neff (2011) is another researcher that investigates the effects of self-compassion and self-appreciation on well-being. According to Neff, self-compassion includes the following three characteristics:

- The ability to be caring and kind to yourself, even in the face of your weaknesses, failures, illness, pain, or unpleasant emotions;
- An understanding of the fact that pain and discomfort are shared human experiences. We all have to deal with adversity, and we all make mistakes. We are all in the same boat; and
- The ability to stay attentive and kind when faced with unpleasant emotions and experiences.

Self-compassion, in other words, is about being kind to yourself unconditionally, and to be attentive to life's discomforts: Do not run away from them, but realize that they are part of the human condition. Among other things, this means being compassionate towards your weaknesses. Self-compassion does not mean repressing unpleasant experiences; it means supporting yourself through adversity in a caring way.

The results of the scientific investigations by researchers such as Gilbert and Neff can be summarized as follows. People with greater self-compassion:

- Are less prone to feelings of fear, sadness, irritation, uncertainty, and stress, and the unpleasant feelings are felt less intensely and more briefly when they do occur;
- Are less prone to repressing unpleasant experiences (thoughts and emotions), and are prepared to weather these experiences, because they are able to support themselves through these experiences;
- Worry less, because they do not try to repress unpleasant experiences;
- Experience greater happiness and optimism;
- Are more appreciative of themselves and the good things in life;
- Are better able to sense what is and is not right for them, and therefore more frequently choose the things that give them joy;
- Show themselves during social engagements because they are not afraid of rejection;
- Are less afraid of failure, and deal with failure more easily;
- Experience greater connection because they are less fixated on their weaknesses, and are able to visualize their place in a greater context (life, humanity);
- Have greater emotional intelligence, meaning they are better able to retain their emotional balance if they are threatened to be thrown off. When confronted with problems, they are able to remain calm and find it easy to adapt, knowing that their problems are not different to those experienced by others. This even shows in the fact that their cortisol levels (stress hormones) are lower when faced with adversity;
- Are better able to learn new skills, because they are prepared to make mistakes. In contrast to self-critical people, it is not fear but love that is the force driving them to learn, and they have no need to prove themselves. These people generally experience more enjoyment during the learning process, and are generally less focused on results; and

- Are better able to be compassionate toward others, and find it easier to forgive other people, meaning that they do not hold grudges.

Self-appreciation

Self-appreciation can be seen as an extension of self-compassion. This appreciation means viewing yourself as a valuable human being, just as you are. You realize that, just like everybody else, you have your weaknesses and you make mistakes; you are satisfied with parts of you that are mediocre; you are happy with and enjoy your strengths. This self-appreciation might be mistaken for overinflated self-esteem, but there is a fundamental difference. In psychology (and in education), attention is paid to problems connected to low self-esteem, and attempts are made to improve this self-esteem. Low self-esteem can lead to complaints, such as fear and depression. Improving self-esteem comes with a few caveats. First, interventions aimed at improving self-esteem are often aimed at combatting weaknesses; a process which, in the end, does not provide enjoyment or energy. We covered this in greater detail in Chapter 2. Second, self-esteem is determined by looking at other people, meaning that there is a risk of lowering your impression of others and/or overinflating your impression of yourself in order to improve your own self-esteem. This is a precarious starting point for change, because the self-image becomes dependent on its comparison to others, with your self-esteem plummeting as soon as you come across people who are better at something than you are.

Self-appreciation, on the other hand, is deriving pride and joy from your strengths just as you are accepting of your weaknesses, knowing that none of us is perfect. This self-appreciation does not come at the cost of your views of others, because you can appreciate them for who they are and do not need to undermine them to feel better about yourself. This has a positive influence on interpersonal relations, and, for example, in working life, will bring out the best in a team.

As early as the first century AD, the philosopher Epictetus described why no human being should let their self-image (and appreciation of others) depend on a comparison to others, because this is a fruitless endeavour. Your traits were gifted to you through heredity, aptitude, social environment, and upbringing. These are not personal achievements, but happenstance and luck. Epictetus wrote:

> These reasonings are unconnected: "I am richer than you, therefore I am better"; "I am more eloquent than you, therefore I am better." The connection is rather this: "I am richer than you, therefore my property is greater than yours;" "I am more eloquent than you, therefore my style is better than yours." But you, after all, are neither property nor style. (Epictetus 2011, p. 58)

Developing compassion for oneself – exercises

The following exercises invite you to be kinder to yourself, and to be so more often. These are exercises which can be done in times of hardship, but it makes sense to familiarize yourself with them beforehand, turning them into a habit.

Exercise 1: Stop self-criticizing and appreciate yourself for who you are

This exercise is aimed at reinforcing the intention to be friendlier towards yourself. This improves the frequency with which the recovery system in your brain is activated.

It may seem pat, but this is essentially the key: Stop criticizing yourself. Stop bringing yourself down. It is a habit that will never make you happy. Pay attention to what you tell yourself. Are these the kinds of things you would dare say to a friend? Self-criticism can be utterly cruel.

Of course, you cannot change a cultivated and culturally determined habit at the flick of a switch. So, stop judging yourself if you are ever critical of yourself. Your intention to stop self-criticizing will make an actual difference. The intention is to appreciate yourself for who you are. This does not mean becoming lazy, or not addressing yourself to take action. It is about reducing to zero the type of self-criticism that is an attack on yourself. Why would you put yourself under siege?

Initially, you will become quicker to notice episodes of self-criticism. These are probably moments during which you are confronted with your weaknesses, pain, or adversity, generating unpleasant emotions (fear, sadness, anger). Ask yourself: Is it my intention to come at myself this hard? Can I allow myself to be kinder to myself? Do I fully realize that, just like any other person, I make mistakes and I have weaknesses?

There is a clip on YouTube that features American actor and stand-up comedian Bob Newhart. In it he plays a psychiatrist who applies the 'Stop it!' method. You can find it by searching for the keywords *Bob Newhart stop it* on YouTube. It is, of course, impossible to repress your thoughts. Even self-criticizing thoughts cannot be controlled in this fashion. Once you realize what an odd thing it is to tell yourself off, you can playfully remind yourself of this advice. If ever you notice a self-criticizing thought rearing its head, just tell yourself: 'Stop it!'

Exercise 2: Wish yourself the best

This exercise involves consciously wishing yourself good things. This reinforces the calming system, and restores balance to the three emotion regulation systems. This exercise may feel a bit awkward or soft, but it is a useful tool for reinforcing your self-compassion.

Once you realize how subversive a self-critical attitude really is, you may experience feelings of sadness, or remember past events, for example, if you did not experience much love during your childhood, or if you were often criticized. If this should happen, you should first allow these emotions to air. Page 99 describes an exercise that allows you to give room to unpleasant emotions.

Have a seat, get comfortable, and relax. Experience the way you are sitting down, and realize that you are a human being with vulnerabilities and strengths. Realize that life is full of positive experiences, but that you will have to endure some set-backs. Let this fact sink in. This is part of being human.

Ask yourself what it is that you need right now. What do you want it for? Do you need relaxation, rest, kindness, security, happiness, health? Allow whatever word best describes your current needs to surface.

Now wish yourself the fulfilment of this need. Wishing it does not mean forcing it. Your wish may or may not be granted, but there is nothing wrong with wishing good upon yourself.

For the next few minutes, say your wish in your head. For example: 'I wish rest for myself, I wish rest for myself, I wish rest for myself.' Some people find it helps to do this in time with their breathing, but this is not required.

Since it is a known fact that a loving touch of the skin will help release the hormone oxytocin, lightly touching yourself can help. For example, placing a hand on the area around your heart, placing both hands on your upper arms, or caressing them. This touch can help you calm down.

End the exercise after a few minutes.

Fredrickson et al. (2008) conducted research into a compassion training course for employees at a large IT company. Participants were invited to take part in various exercises, such as focusing their attention on the area around their heart, and then thinking of someone they cared about. They were then asked to expand their attention to themselves and others (see Exercises 7 and 8 in Chapter 7). The training uses thoughts and visualizations whose goal is to stimulate pleasant emotions, such as love, satisfaction, and compassion. A group of 102 employees took part in six sessions of sixty minutes each; a group of 100 others was placed on a waiting list. Results indicated that participants experienced a gradual increase of pleasant emotions in training; for people on the waiting list, levels of pleasant emotions remained the same. It was also demonstrated that the increase in pleasant emotions experienced daily had a positive effect on life goals and social support, while reducing the number of health complaints. This had additional effects on life satisfaction experiences. Follow-up research conducted fifteen months later showed that the effects experienced by participants in the training were retained (Cohn et al., 2009).

Exercise 3: The 'granny-exercise'

This exercise uses your imagination. Thoughts and imaginations influence our brain's response. The threat system is activated by our imagination in no-time, for example, if we imagine we are in danger. This same ability is addressed in this exercise, but here as a way of activating our calming system.

Imagine someone you know or knew who always has or had your best interest at heart. You may have (had) a loving grandmother, who was always there for you in times of trouble. It could be anyone, such as a father, mother, neighbour, or teacher. Alternatively, you can imagine a person who radiates compassion, if you prefer. This can be someone you know personally, or someone you know from TV.

Imagine that person is here now, being kind to you. Use your fantasy and imagination. What is this person doing? Have they put their arm around you? How do they look at you? What are they saying? Feel the energy of this flow through you. What do you feel?

There is nothing magical about this exercise; you are not generating energies or contacting the dearly departed. It works the same as when you imagine something that frightens you, which is to say by activating a system in your brain. For these compassionate images, it is your calming system that is activated.

Exercise 4: Fan the flame of kindness within

Take a notepad. For the next five minutes, write down situations during which you were kind to yourself and/or someone else this week. It does not matter how big or small, how ordinary or exceptional. For example: asking a colleague about their day, complimenting a child, helping an elderly person cross the street, letting someone have your seat on a bus, addressing yourself positively, donating to charity, driving a colleague home who was feeling poorly, comforting the parents of a child with learning disabilities, tussling with your dog, or giving your partner a bunch of flowers.

Reflect on how these situations affected yourself and the other person(s). How did they respond, and how did you feel? Reflect on the kindness within yourself. What do these situations tell you about yourself as a person?

Exercise 5: Welcome everything, suppressing nothing

This exercise is aimed at recognizing unpleasant emotions. We tend to suppress or avoid unpleasant emotions, because these are experiences we do not tend to enjoy. Nevertheless, these experiences are part of our life, and we damage ourselves by not letting them in. First, because rejecting unpleasant experiences makes us feel even worse. Second, because this will also lead us to close off from pleasant experiences as well, since it is impossible to reject unpleasantness exclusively. We have come up with so many ways of evading the things we do not enjoy, such as addictive behaviour (excessive eating, drinking, sex, drug use) and avoidance behaviour (avoiding situations which, for example, inspire fear).

Earlier we described how self-compassion and love are all-encompassing experiences, which can coexist alongside feelings of fear, anger or sadness. The goal of compassion is not to suppress other feelings, but to recognize that something is hard *and* to face it with kindness.

This is an exercise you can do if you are confronted by fear, anger, or sadness.

1. Allow the feeling to exist. How does it make you feel, physically? If you find yourself thinking about how this

feeling came to be, then try to leave the 'story' of the emotions for what it is. Experience how the pain or emotion is expressing itself in your body as a form of energy. Your throat, your chest, your stomach: these are often the areas where emotions are felt the most. What do they feel like: oppressive, restrictive, large, small, sharp, hard, burning, freezing, prickling? You may feel as though the emotions are expressing themselves in certain shapes, or certain colours. Allow these images to surface.

2. Tell yourself: 'This sadness, this fear, or this anger is difficult for me and it is permitted', and touch yourself lightly (hand near your heart, or hands on your upper arms). If you find it comforting to do so, remember the Granny-exercise; imagine someone who has your best interest at heart – a loving granny, a friend, a parent, a partner. What would this person say to you right now?

3. Keep track of what is happening to your body. Allow the feelings to become stronger, to increase, to reduce. Whatever they do, allow it.

4. As soon as you notice that you start to wander and begin looking for explanations for your anger, sadness, or fear, then try to let go of this 'story' and refocus on the energy in your body.

5. Repeat to yourself: 'This is permitted', and touch yourself lightly.

6. Take as long as you want to allow the feelings to exist.

References

Cohn, M.A., Fredrickson, B.L., Brown, S.L., Mikels, J.A., and Conway, A.M. (2009). Happiness unpacked: Positive emotions increase life satisfaction by building resilience. *Emotion*, 9, 361–368.

Epictetus (2011). *Zakboekje: wenken voor een evenwichtig leven.* Amsterdam: Boom uitgevers Amsterdam.

Fredrickson, B.L., Cohn, M.A., Coffey, K.A., Pek, J., and Finkel, S.M. (2008). Open hearts build lives: Positive emotions, induced through loving-kindness meditation, build consequential personal resources. *Journal of Personality and Social Psychology, 95*, 1045–1062.

Gilbert, P.G. (2009). *The compassionate mind.* London: Constable.

Gilbert, P.G., and Choden (2013). *Mindful compassion: Using the power of mindfulness and compassion to transform our lives.* London: Constable & Robinson Ltd.

Neff, K. (2011). *Self-compassion: Stop beating yourself up and leave insecurity behind.* New York: HarperCollins Publishers.

Chapter 6

I am not who I once was

Introduction

At the end of the twentieth century, psychologists Chris Peterson and Martin Seligman (2003) published the results of a large-scale study conducted across four-thousand Americans. They asked in what way their subjects experienced specific strengths. At the time, the researchers could not have imagined the ill-fated events of September 11, 2001 that were about to unfold. Two aeroplanes struck New York's Twin Towers, resulting in the loss of thousands of lives. This was a profound and traumatic event for many Americans, and not just for those directly involved or their next of kin. Ten months on, the researchers wonder how their test subjects had experienced their strengths in the wake of the event. They decided to ask the same people to fill in the same questionnaire again. As it turned out, participants now scored higher in strengths like gratitude, hope, kindness, leadership skills, love, faith, and collegiality. These effects remained noticeable for longer.

When confronted with a serious life event, all your ideas about pleasant emotions, experiencing daily life to the fullest, and growing as a person seem to drop away. And initially, they do. The confrontation with a life-threatening situation (illness, violence, accidents, natural disasters) is harrowing, pointless, and raw. All meaning is lost. Nevertheless, countless research shows that the majority of people later indicated that their traumatic experience caused them to grow. This tells us something about humanity's incredible flexibility and capacity for survival. We are apparently able to take the pain and the sadness that inevitably comes with any profound or overwhelming event, and turn them into something else, to flip them, to transform them. This makes us experience greater strength or 'improvement' as a result of the confrontation.

In the field of positive psychology, this is known as 'post-traumatic growth', and there have been hundreds of investigations into its process, such as that mentioned above. This chapter is about post-traumatic stress and growth. How do we explain post-traumatic growth? And what can you do to transform an invasive or traumatic experience? This chapter talks about traumatic experiences. But that which applies to trauma, also applies to adversity and stressful living conditions. Even if you have never suffered through something traumatic, the following text can also be read from the context of a stressful event or difficult circumstances.

The results of dramatic life events

Post-traumatic stress

Whenever we are confronted with a traumatic event, this is a highly invasive experience. Traumatic events are so far removed from our normal, every-day experiences, that they shock us to our core. The ideas about what constitutes trauma have changed over the years. Until around 20 years ago, an event was considered a trauma if (almost) anyone who experienced it would have been shocked and overcome. Experiences that were referred to in terms of trauma were considered to be those that were extreme and exceptional, such as living through a natural disaster or fighting in a war.

As of the 1990s, however, the definition of 'traumatic' has shifted to include subjective experience and perception.

Psychologists refer to 'trauma' to indicate someone has experienced an event where death or possibility of dying, severe injury, or a threat to physical integrity played a role. And when someone responds to this event with fear, hopelessness, or terror. It is now fully recognized that events like abuse, assault, rape, traffic accidents, life-threatening illnesses, or medical operations can be traumatic.

Living through a traumatic event has a huge impact. Mental consequences resulting from such an event are known as 'post-traumatic stress'. Post-traumatic stress encompasses four types of symptoms:

1. Intrusion: The event is relived time and time again. Images, thoughts, and feelings invade your consciousness and lead to intense emotions, such as fear, panic, terror, and grief. Intrusions can also occur in the form of flashbacks or nightmares.
2. Avoidance: You continually tend to avoid anything that may remind you of the event, such as feelings, people, certain locations or activities. Memories are repressed, and emotions are flattened or superficial. You find it hard to experience normal feelings such as happiness or pride, and you do not feel involved with other people or society.
3. A negative change to your thoughts and mood caused by the traumatic event: Examples include having a negative view of yourself, others, or the world in general; persist distorted thoughts about the cause, such as blaming yourself; persistent unpleasant emotions, such as anger, fear, or disgust; a reduced interest in taking part in activities.
4. Increased irritability: This can manifest as physical characteristics, such as rapid breathing, sweating, or heart palpitations. You are more easily agitated, and may experience aggression of bouts of rage. You feel a heightened sense of alertness, causing you to be on guard continually.

Experiencing these symptoms during the initial period following a traumatic event is quite normal. It is part of processing an overwhelming experience. At first, the experience can also be denied or repressed. Subsequently, the experience is admitted and processed bit by bit. Many people see a reduction in stress symptoms as a sign that the experience has been processed. In others, the symptoms remain or increase in frequency or severity. Processing the event stagnates, leading to a post-traumatic stress disorder. In that case, the best thing to do is to find help, for example through cognitive behavioural therapy, or EMDR (Eye Movement Desensitization and Reprocessing). These types of treatments are effective in dealing with post-traumatic stress complaints – and finding help when we need it is also a compassionate thing to do. Dealing with and processing stress is quite a feat, but it is an important condition to arrive at a positive destination.

Transformation following a traumatic event

What exactly defines an event as 'traumatic'? The event you experienced was shocking, but what part of you, precisely, did it shock? Human beings who grow up in a (reasonably) safe and loving environment develop a number of basic convictions about the world we live in (Janoff-Bulman, 1992). The first conviction is that the world is kind, and that nothing can happen to us. We assume that the chance of experiencing something positive is greater than that of experiencing something negative. The second conviction is that the world is predictable, verifiable, and meaningful. We believe that, eventually, positive and healthy conduct and effort will be rewarded. The third conviction is that, in principle, we are doing the right things. We tend to view our behaviour and intentions in a positive light. We trust that we are virtuous. In general, we tend to overestimate our influence on the world. But we need these convictions to live, to actively contribute.

The shocking part of a traumatic event is that it turns these basic convictions, the ones that lend us such support, upside down. Psychologists Tedeschi and Calhoun, who performed a lot of research into post-traumatic growth, therefore compare a traumatic event to an earthquake. It causes our basic faith in the world to become unsteady. All at once we are forced to deal with how fragile and mortal we really are. And with how fickle and unjust the world can be. Aside from the intense emotions and intrusions we experience following a traumatic event, we also have to process it cognitively. How do we explain that this happened to us? How can we make this event meaningful? What should be our view of the world after this? What should we believe in? What convictions can be still held true? We are asked to think about the meaning of the event. Psychologists call this 'ruminating', like a cow chewing the cud. We can distinguish between two types of ruminating:

The first type of ruminating can also be called 'worrying'. Worrying is about blame and cause. The first questions following a traumatic event are often concerned with our disbelief about what has happened to us. Why did this happen to me? Could it have gone differently? Could I have done something to prevent it? We think about what caused the event, and what our part in it has been. This kind of ruminating does not help us move on; we keep going around in circles.

The second type of ruminating could be called 'reflecting'. Reflecting is about finding meaning and about learning. How can I deal with this? What does it teach me? How can I (re)shape my life based on my experiences? This type of ruminating does help us move on; it eventually liberates us and presents us with the possibility of a future in which we have given room to the traumatic event.

Joseph (2011), another psychologist who conducted a lot of research into post-traumatic growth, compares rebuilding your life and your convictions to a broken vase. A vase that is broken into two or three pieces can often be restored by gluing the pieces together. The breaks may be hardly if at all noticeable; it may almost be impossible to tell that this is no longer a pristine vase. But if the vase is shattered into a hundred fragments, gluing them together becomes impossible. You can get bogged down and frustrated in your attempts to restore the vase to its original state. And even if, through some miracle, you did manage to put the thing back together again, anyone who looked at it would see that something had happened to it. The alternative? Do something new with the fragments you have. A mosaic, for example, is a way of transforming the vase into something new.

Joseph places post-traumatic growth within the humanist vision of human development, as discussed in the introduction to this book. Under the right conditions, human beings grow and flourish. Normally, this is a more gradual process. Using your life experience, everything you encounter throughout your years, you may come to realize new insights and convictions about life. Note the operative word here is 'may', because we can also be conservative in our convictions about the world and ourselves. One of our 'dated' convictions can still feel so familiar that we find it hard to let go of. A traumatic event suddenly and rapidly accelerates this process. You are forced to revise your notions and convictions. You can no longer be who you were before the event(s) occurred. If you try (which is understandable), you will run aground – your life will stagnate.

One of the ways to hold on to your basic convictions about a verifiable, predictable, and benevolent world, is to blame yourself. If you try to convince yourself that you could have been the one to prevent the traumatic event from happening, that you should have seen it coming and that you should have made different choices, then you can hold on to your idea of a kind and predictable world. But at what cost? From that moment on, you will live your life under a tremendous burden; a burden of guilt and self-criticism. And that is no basis for a good life.

If you find room to process a shocking event as part of your natural tendency to grow and blossom, you can view the ruminating process and an important part to the process of post-traumatic growth. Ruminating is not just a part of the stress response, something you had better get rid of quickly. You need to ruminate, and particularly to reflect, in order to revaluate your life, to process your experiences into new notions and convictions, to make something new out of the fragmented vase. By its very nature this process is be a painful struggle. But without it, you will become bogged down in your inability to accept, in your feeling of impotence, in your self-criticism. Instead, taking part in a ruminating process will lead you to recognize that the experience has altered you. It will help you look for and find new convictions, and you will come to find that your life has transformed as a result. This transformation is known as 'post-traumatic growth', which raises the question: What does this growth look like?

Aspects of post-traumatic growth

Listening to stories told by people who have experienced trauma, and asking them how they have grown, you will find that they all describe different growth domains (Tedeschi and Calhoun, 2004): life in general, relationships, personal strengths, new perspectives, and spirituality.

- Life in general: A greater appreciation for life, greater appreciation for the 'little things' that are part of daily life, different priorities, gratefulness to be alive;
- Relationships: A deeper sense of connectedness to important others, greater love and empathy towards others, greater intimacy;
- Personal strengths: A greater awareness of personal strengths, increased awareness of fragility, combined with greater self-confidence and power;
- New perspectives: A clearer understanding of life goals, beginning new education, powerfully inspired; and
- Spirituality: Greater religious conviction, increased interest in existential and philosophical questions, increased attention to spiritual development.

Benefits and obstructions to post-traumatic growth

Two factors play a major role in the occurrence of post-traumatic growth: flexible coping and self-determination.

Flexible coping

There has been a lot of research into the factors that improve or hinder post-traumatic growth (Joseph, 2011). This is done by investigating how people cope with the stress caused by a traumatic event. In the field of psychology, this is known as 'coping', with an important distinction between 'avoidant coping' and 'process-oriented coping'. Avoidant coping involves, for example, trying to avoid anything that may remind you of a certain event, and suppressing the emotions and thoughts about the event as much as possible.

Examples of avoidant coping are:

- Denial: Pretending nothing has happened; letting things get back to normal as soon as possible;
- Disbelief with what happened to you;
- Worrying from the false conviction that you can regain control of the situation;
- Getting lost in your work to avoid experiencing the emotions that remind you of the event;
- Not wanting to talk about it;
- Refusing to work on your recovery;
- Resorting to excess alcohol or other narcotics; and
- Avoiding situations or people that may remind you of the event.

In the first few days following the traumatic event, avoidance and denial are normal responses that can actually help you protect yourself. The experience has been so overwhelming as to make it impossible to have them sink in straight away. But if avoidant behaviour becomes a long-term strategy, it hinders (or even prevents) proper processing, and increases your chances of experiencing stress-related complaints. There is a major chance that you will become caught in a negative spiral, resulting in deteriorating health, alienation of others, and developing psychological complaints such as depression and fear.

Process-oriented coping

At some point in your life, you need to come to terms with the situation in order to move on. This process of actively getting to terms with something, or 'process-oriented coping', distinguishes between 'task-oriented coping' and 'emotion-oriented coping'.

Task-oriented coping involves all the practical matters that need taking care of. If you have been physically injured, your living arrangements may require some adjustments. You may need physiotherapy sessions; you may need to learn how to use an artificial limb. Task-oriented coping also includes making adjustments to your life goals. It has to do with facing reality: What are my real limitations and possibilities? How do I proceed to give my life meaning from here on out? Being optimistic and hopeful, as covered in Chapter 4, plays an important part in this.

Emotion-oriented coping is aimed at processing what you have experienced. Expressing your feelings, talking about them to others who will support you are examples of this form of coping. Crucial to emotion-oriented coping is that the type of support corresponds to your personal needs. People who are compassionate or good at listening, without providing unsolicited advice or solutions, are of great value. They will provide you with the space you need to tell your story and express yourself. Self-compassion, the ability to permit yourself to experience negative emotions and being kind and loving towards yourself, strongly contributes to emotion-oriented coping. But experiencing levity can also help you process the event: A sense of humour and the ability to experience pleasant emotions during times of difficulty have proven to be important factors in the development of post-traumatic growth. In addition, many people are able to draw support from their faith.

Self-determination

There is a second important condition to transforming and experiencing personal growth. Whereas coping refers to your actual behaviour, this second factor is to do with your basic attitude and intentions. People who experience a traumatic event have, as a result, become victims. Something happened to them, something terrible, something they did not choose to experience. As a victim, it makes perfect sense that they would be upset by this, and that they now feel powerless. What happened should not have happened. It is unjust, it is tragic. Feeling victimized is perfectly justified.

But the questions we all have to answer if we ever find ourselves in this situation are: What comes next? Will I let this event dictate what happens with the rest of my life? There are two options. The first is to let your role of victim take over your life. It becomes the whole of your identity. In essence, this is saying: 'My circumstances determine who I am. I am dependent and powerless. This happened to me even though it should not have.' You place the responsibility for your life outside yourself. If this is your internal attitude, you will generally become passive and helpless. Your past will begin to determine your future. You ruminate mainly in the form of worry and self-pity. The question is: Does this make you feel good? Is this the person you wish to be?

Post-traumatic growth becomes possible as you flick the switch of your inner attitude to a different position over time: The position of self-determiner. A self-determiner eventually comes to readjust their view of the situation to what it is now, and looking for new possibilities and meanings in this current context. Self-determiners ruminate on the basis of reflection. Their strength is in giving new meaning to whatever situation they are now in. Self-determiners keep setting themselves new challenges and new goals. This is not the same as saying that they do not know sadness or anger. Someone who is a self-determiner is just as much a victim, and can feel just as overwhelmed. But that is not where the feelings end. The self-determiner is the one who restores purpose to their own life, instead of letting circumstances dictate their purpose for them. The present and the future become deciding factors in their life. They are able to envision a future that inspires them, and to commit to making that future a reality. Martin Luther King Jr., Nelson Mandela, and Viktor Frankl were all examples of people who, even in the toughest of circumstances, persevered in their self-determination, in finding meaning in their situation. This has made them a source of enormous inspiration to many people. The text below discusses some of the important insights by neurologist and psychiatrist Viktor Frankl, a survivor of the Nazi's concentration camps in World War II.

VIKTOR FRANKL, NEUROLOGIST AND PSYCHIATRIST (1905–1997)[1]

Victor Frankl describes how, based on his experiences as a prisoner in the concentration camps of Nazi-Germany, he came to realize that human beings – even in times of great suffering – retain their freedom in how they relate to their circumstances.

> Man is not fully conditioned and determined but rather determines himself whether he gives in to conditions or stands up to them. In other words, man is ultimately self-determining. (1978, p. 159)

Frankl found that a number of factors play a role in our capacity for mental health and self-determination: love, finding meaning in our own lives, recognizing our own responsibility, and having a hopeful outlook on the future.

Love

Frankl describes how, during the cold marches to the working site, he would visualize his wife, and hear her voice:

> A thought transfixed me: for the first time in my life I saw the truth [. . .] The truth – that love is the ultimate and the highest goal to which man can aspire [. . .] In a position of utter desolation, when man cannot express himself in positive action, when his only achievement may consist in enduring his sufferings in the right way – an honourable way – in such a position man can, through loving contemplation of the image he carries of his beloved, achieve fulfilment. (1978, p.55)

And:

> I knew only one thing – which I have learned well by now: Love goes very far beyond the physical person of the beloved. It finds its deepest meaning in his spiritual being, his inner self. (1978, p. 56)

Recognizing Our Own Responsibility

We, as human beings, always retain our ability to choose. That choice: What is the relationship between what is inside us and what is outside us?

> Life ultimately means taking the responsibility to find the right answer to its problems and to fulfil the tasks which it constantly sets for each individual. (1978, p. 99)
>
> What he becomes – within the limits of endowment and environment – he has made out of himself. In the concentration camps, for example, in this living laboratory and on this testing ground, we watched and witnessed some of our comrades behave like swines while others behaved like saints. Man has both potentialities within himself; which one is actualized depends on decisions but not on conditions. (1978, p. 163)

Finding meaning in our lives

Frankl describes how the chances of surviving in the concentration camp seemed greater for people who understood the meaning of their lives, even in these times of great suffering. It is not possible to define the meaning of life, since every human being's destination is unique. At the core of the treatment he later developed (known as 'logotherapy') is the idea that we must give meaning to our own lives, and find a reason to live. Frankl describes how many people suffer from an existential vacuum, a feeling that existence is pointless, leading them to try to fill this inner void with power, money, or sex.

Faith in a future goal

Another important observation by Frankl was that people who gave up hope for the future were the ones to succumb to illnesses and death. He describes several cases in which he observed this connection in fellow prisoners.

> It is a peculiarity of man that he can only live by looking to the future ... [. . .] The prisoner who had lost faith in the future – his future – was doomed. With his loss of belief in the future, he also lost his spiritual hold. [. . .] any attempt to restore a man's inner strength in the camp had first to succeed in showing him some future goal. (1978, pp. 95–96)

Trying circumstances

What applies to traumatic events to some degree also applies to experiences that may be less invasive but are still stressful. The major difference is that, for traumatic events, all of one's handles on and convictions about life fall away at once. A traumatic event is sudden, a shock. This may not be the case for stressful situations, but you can also grow in the face of adversity. Daily events can be very stressful, especially those that compound: caring for a child or other family member who is ill, problems at work, poor achievements at school, worrying child behaviour, debts, conflicts, etc.

Everything we have explained about coping also applies to these situations: You can assume the role of victim, or you can be accepting and look for meaningful answers, challenging yourself to be, as the US army would have it, all that you can be. These are also situations which you can look back on as points where you changed as a person, that they helped you grow, made you wiser, or milder. Or that they brought you closer to others, made you re-evaluate your priorities and appreciate certain things more.

Growing in the face of trauma or adversity – exercises

Before you proceed with the following exercises, we recommend that you take a look at the following list of complaints. If you are suffering from one or more of these complaints, we recommend that you consult your GP or look for other forms of professional guidance.

- You feel overwhelmed by emotions;
- You feel drained or numb;
- You feel very tense or exhausted;
- You are having nightmares;
- You are having sexual issues;
- You drink alcohol or use narcotics excessively;

- You keep trying to avoid thoughts, places, and people that remind you of an event; and
- You experience problems in your daily life, for example, in relationships or at work, or you feel abandoned.

The following exercises can help you free up room for personal growth following a traumatic event or other form of adversity. But this cannot be forced. Recovering from a traumatic event or from adversity is a process. There will be ups and downs. These exercises can help you strike a balance between making room for negative emotions on the one hand, and refocusing your attention on positive experiences on the other.

The first two exercises are meant to help you get an insight into what type of coping you apply. Next, you can discover whether there are more helpful coping styles you can address or develop.

Exercise 1: Coping patterns

The following is an overview of possible coping styles.

If you recently experienced a traumatic or troubling event, or if you are currently experiencing a lot of stress: Consider the way in which you dealt or are dealing with it.

If the traumatic or troubling event did not happen recently, consider the period during and directly following it. For each coping style, check the boxes to indicate to what extent you employ the methods listed. It is possible that you find it hard to visualize the different coping styles, or that you find it hard to be honest about certain things. If that is the case, you should consider having this questionnaire filled in by someone who knows you well.

Table 6.1 Coping patterns

	Rarely/ not at all	Some- times	Often	Very often
Avoidant coping				
Denial: Pretending nothing has happened				
Disbelief with what happened to you				
Worrying from the false conviction that you can regain control of the situation				
Getting lost in your work to avoid experiencing the emotions that remind you of the event				
Not wanting to talk about it				
Refusing to work on your recovery				
Resorting to excess alcohol or other narcotics				
Avoiding situations or people that may remind you of the event				
Process-oriented coping				
Looking for healthy distractions				
Looking for practical aid				
Taking up day-to-day activities				
Facing and actively dealing with your problems				
Physical exercise				
Expressing your emotions to yourself				
Looking for emotional support				
Talking about your experiences				
Trying to find the positive aspects				
Appreciating what is there				
Turning to your faith for support				
Joking, looking for levity				

What do you notice? Which of these emotion-oriented coping styles do you use rarely or not at all? Which of the avoidant coping styles do you use often or very often? What patterns can you identify with yourself?

Does your coping speak to the victim role, or are you working from self-determination? Have you made the adjustments required by the situation?

You should realize that these coping styles are not necessarily good or bad. The challenge is in being flexible with which coping styles you apply; they depend on your situation, who you are with, what you need at a specific time. You can identify whether you are caught in a certain pattern, recognize it with kindness and compassion, and then try out new behaviours – scary though they may seem.

Exercise 2: Change your coping pattern(s)

This exercise applies if the outcome of Exercise 1 indicates that there are avoidant coping styles you apply often or very often, or process-oriented coping styles you apply rarely or never at all.

Choose which coping style you want to address first. Apply what you learned about setting goals, planning actions, and being optimistic and hopeful in Chapters 3 and 4:

- Formulate a concrete goal and concrete actions (when, with whom, how, what; answer these questions for your intended goal and actions);
- Visualize your actions before executing them; and
- If at first you do not (entirely) succeed, then focus on what went right. Consider what you would need to improve your next effort.

The following exercises can help to support your emotion-oriented coping. Choose and regularly do whichever one(s) you feel are helpful or comfortable.

Exercise 3: Self-compassion

For this exercise, refer to Exercise 5 in Chapter 5: 'Welcome everything, suppressing nothing' on page 99. This exercise helps you give room to your unpleasant emotions in a kind manner. By allowing your emotions to air, you can begin to process them. This is a good exercise if you tend to suppress or dull your emotions, or if you tend to keep distracting yourself from the coping process.

Exercise 4: Expressive writing

For at least four days, take 15 minutes every day to write about your experiences. Write about what happened to you. But, above all, write about your deepest, most hidden emotions, thoughts, and feelings. If you find this hard to do, begin by writing about positive events you experience; this may be easier for people who tend to apply avoidant coping strategies.

There have been dozens of studies into the effects of expressive writing. Many of them show that expressive writing can lead to fewer complaints and fewer GP visits. A study of breast cancer patients (Stanton et al., 2002) demonstrated that people who wrote about their emotions, thoughts, and positive experiences over the course of a week experienced less fear and sadness, and were also less likely to visit GPs or hospitals than the people who were asked to write about their actual illness.

Exercise 5: Three good things

During difficult times, it is vitally important to pay attention to and make room for pleasant emotions as well. This will help you enhance your resilience, covered in Chapter 1 on pleasant emotions. At the end of every day, take five minutes to consider what went well, what positive things you experienced. Were there moments of pride, gratitude, calmness, love, of different emotions? What did you experience? Take some time out of your day to recall and relive that moment.

The following exercises are aimed at reinforcing your self-determination. Choose and regularly do whichever one(s) you feel are helpful or comfortable.

Exercise 6: What does my situation require of me?

You have lived through an invasive event, or you are currently in a difficult situation. Answer the following questions:

- What does my situation require of me?
- Which of my strengths can I apply and continue to develop?

Exercise 7: Good advice

Imagine yourself in ten years. You are wiser now than you were. Looking back on this period of your life, what would your older-self recommend to the you of back then? What can you show them? What can you come up with?

Exercise 8: Which needs do you experience?

Have a sneak peek at the list of needs on page 140. What do you need right at this moment? Who do you feel should know about your needs? The next chapter discusses how to communicate compassionately.

Exercise 9: Grow stronger

You are experiencing a difficult time. The renowned philosopher Friedrich Nietzsche was a man who also experienced a great deal. He suffered from depressions, physical illnesses, and anxiety. Nietzsche famously wrote: 'That which does not kill us makes us stronger.'

What are you carrying with you? What have your experiences taught you about what is important in life? What are you going to change? How have you grown?

Exercise 10: Reinforce your hope of a happy ending

Imagine yourself three months on; you have been working hard to process the event. Something has changed: You still occasionally experience stress, sadness, or fear, but these things no longer pervade your life. You have done everything in you power to deal with this difficult time wisely and well. You have actively and flexibly applied the various coping styles. You have looked for and found ways of giving meaning to a difficult situation by addressing your power and your wisdom.

Visualize the person you will have become. What are you doing? What do you look like? What do you experience?

Note

1 Based on *Man's search for meaning* (1992).

References

Frankl, V. (1978). *De zin van het bestaan. (Meaning of life)*. Rotterdam: Ad Donker bv.

Janoff-Bulman, R. (1992). *Shattered assumptions: Towards a new psychology of trauma*. New York: The Free Press.

Joseph, S. (2011). *What doesn't kill us: The new psychology of posttraumatic growth*. New York: Basic Books.

Peterson, C., and Seligman, M.E.P. (2003). Character strengths before and after September 11. *Psychological Science, 14*, 381–384.

Stanton, A.L., Danoff-Burg, S., Sworowski, L.A., Collins, C.A., Branstetter, A.D., Rodriguez-Hanley, A., Kirk, S.B., and Austenfeld, J.L. (2002). Randomized, controlled trial of written emotional expression and benefit finding in breast cancer patients. *Journal of Clinical Oncology, 20*, 4160–4168.

Tedeschi, R.G., and Calhoun, L.G. (2004). Posttraumatic growth: Conceptual foundations and empirical evidence. *Psychological Inquiry, 15*, 1–18.

Chapter 7

Sharing your positive life

Introduction

So far, this book has been about you as an individual. About your ability to appreciate what is there, and about the art of enjoying wonderful experiences. About developing your strengths. About imagining a future in which your talents have come to fruition. About taking the steps needed to get you there. About kindness and love for yourself, about processing painful events, and about self-determination. The focus, so far, mainly seems to have been you. But that is not entirely accurate.

This book is about self-realization, which implies transcending self-interest and self-centeredness. Self-realization goes hand-in-hand with attention to others, because we, as human beings, are not isolated – no one is an island unto themselves. We are connected to others. We live in a world which we depend on, and which we are responsible for. Personal growth automatically leads us to make others and the world around us more important. Once you come to understand the needs of others and what you can do for others and the world in general, and once that understanding has become the guiding force in your life, then that is a sign that your self-realization has occurred. Positive relationships, kindness, making an effort for others, experiencing a connection: These are the foundation of well-being, and are among the most impressive experiences imaginable. They are the subjects of the following two chapters.

Two things that are essential to positive living are relationships and communication. Relationships of love, family, friendship, and collegiality are important sources of meaning. We are not isolated, but fundamentally connected to others. Having good relationships with others means being able to express our emotions, show our vulnerabilities, receive support, exchange ideas, celebrate, and mourn. The quality of relationships is essential to our joy in daily life. The field of psychology placed the initial focus on relational conflict and dysfunction. There have also been many studies into the effects of social support and stress and coping with negative life events. In recent years, there has also been attention for optimum relationship functioning. An optimum relationship allows both persons to grow. What are the processes that contribute to an optimum relationship? We will discuss the important role that communication has to play. Taking the time and listening attentively and actively are important characteristics of a positive relationship. As are how we respond to another's positive news and life joy. And how do we communicate compassionately?

Developing positive relationships

Characteristics of positive relationships

We have previously described how autonomy, competence, and connectedness are three fundamental human needs (see Chapter 2). When these needs are met, we flourish. Positive relationships are those relationships in which connectedness is experienced strongly. Scientists who have studied positive relationships extensively, such as Harry Reis and Shelly Gable (2003), differentiate the following characteristics of positive relationships: intimacy, affection, and fun.

Intimacy includes experiencing closeness; showing important aspects of ourselves, such as our fragility and our quality;

paying attention to what the other person is experiencing; mutual understanding and caring. The extent to which partners feel understood and appreciated by their other half is of major influence on the extent to which they experience connectedness.

Affection includes loving touches, sexuality, and attentiveness. The extent to which partners experience affection is an important predictor as to the extent to which partners remain satisfied with a relationship. One of the studies (Huston et al., 2001) into affection showed that the number of marital divorces could be predicted based on the extent to which affection in marriages had been open as much as 13 years earlier. The more affectionate, the greater the chances the relationship would still be ongoing.

Fun includes the communal taking part in enjoyable and new activities. A joint experience of positive feelings, such as excitement, enthusiasm, and inspiration, is a strong contributor to satisfaction and passion in relationships.

Intimacy, affection, and fun can be regarded as an expression of commitment demonstrating the amount of effort either partner is actually willing to invest in a relationship, and the extent to which they are focused on the other half's well-being and growth (Fincham and Beach, 2010). Commitment in a relationship leads to a number of positive interactions and pleasant emotions that are far greater than the negative interactions and unpleasant emotions. As covered in Chapter 1, experiencing pleasant emotions leads to a broadening of attention, an increase in flexibility of behaviour, and to creativity. When a relationship flourishes, so do the partners involved. If you are looking to improve a relationship, you will need to invest in your commitment to that relationship. This can be done by undertaking fun activities, sharing your experiences, and showing affection.

SELF-EXPANSION

Human beings have a powerful need to expand and develop their self-image, and gain a lot of satisfaction from being able to do so (Aron and Aron, 1986). This process is known as self-expansion. Self-expansion can express itself in many ways, as covered in this book: developing your strengths and spirituality, and expressing your creativity. But friendships and intimate relationships offer many possibilities for self-expansion, for example, when you become attentive to some of your partner's or friend's interests. If they have a fascination with Australia, you will learn a lot more about that country than you would otherwise. You may develop a taste for a vacation down under.

Studies (Aron et al., 2000 and Aron and Aron, 1986) have also shown that partners in love tend to assume each other's characteristics and quality, and absorb these into their own self-image. This explains why it so important to continue to share new and inspiring activities. There are numerous opportunities for self-expansion during the first phases of a relationship. You get to know the other person and undertake new, exciting activities together. As time goes on, this happens less frequently. If both partners remain actively pursuant of novelties together, they contribute to each other's self-expansion while at the same time keeping the relationship alive and blossoming.

Sharing positive experiences

If we have good news or if we have experienced something positive, we like to tell our partners, friends, or colleagues about this. Telling others about an enjoyable experience increases the effect of the experience itself. This is also known as 'capitalizing' because it involves getting the most out of (or 'capitalizing on') a positive event. Capitalizing is something we do all the time. Studies have shown that at least 70 per cent of our positive experiences are shared with another party the same day (mostly with our partners, family, or friends). Telling others about positive experiences is shown to have a positive effect on our well-being, an effect that transcends the experience itself. And the more we share the experience, the more potent its effect on our well-being.

It is interesting that our reaction to the positive experiences of others plays a crucial role in the process of capitalizing. Psychologist Shelly Gable developed a questionnaire which distinguishes between four types of responses to other people sharing their positive experiences: active and constructive, passive and constructive, active and destructive, and passive and destructive. Here are some examples of each of these responses applied to a friend talking about his work promotion:

- Active and Constructive
  'That is terrific! I am so proud of you. I know you worked hard to get that promotion; it is very well earned. Let's celebrate later – I must know everything. When did you hear, what were you doing? What did your supervisor say, exactly?'
- Passive and Constructive
  'That is good news. Congratulations!'
- Active and Destructive
  'Gosh, that is good news, but are you sure you are ready? And how does your wife feel about this? You are away from home often enough as it is.'
- Passive and Destructive
  'Right. Hey, I read about this new movie. Want to go there tonight?'

At the core of an active and constructive response is that you display your feelings of enthusiasm and happiness. Your intention is to celebrate, and to have the other person share all the details so that you can both relive the event together. This response is born from empathic joy: You imagine yourself in your friend's situation, experiencing their happiness, and show your involvement through your questions and non-verbal posture. Empathic joy can be compared to general compassion, which means imaging yourself in the situation of someone who is in difficulty, and who you support by showing your compassion.

Gable et al. (2004) studied couples who had been dating for several months, as well as married couples. They found that both men and women who felt their partner generally responded actively/constructively were more satisfied with their relationships. These men and women experienced greater feelings of intimacy and trust. The other three types of responses, even the passive/constructive type, lead to decreased satisfaction, intimacy, and trust.

Another study interviewed people on a positive event in their lives (Reis et al., 2010). In group A, the interviewers were assigned with responding actively/constructively; in group B, they were told to react passively/constructively. A week after the interview, participants in group A indicated they felt more connected to their interviewers than the members of group B. An important aspect of the effectiveness of and active/constructive response is that the storyteller feels truly understood regarding what they feel is important.

Active listening

An active and constructive response is a form of active listening. Active listening means focusing all of your attention on what the other party is saying, and giving them the space to tell their story. You try to discern the essence of their story and their underlying feelings, and show them that you understand what they are telling you. There is an art to actively listening, and that is in not passing judgement or giving criticism unless the other party asks you to. Active listening does not involve, for example, criticizing, praising, providing solutions, advising, comforting, and reasoning logically. A study by Driver and Gottman (2004) showed that happy partners responded to each other attentively and positively in 85 per cent of cases. The researchers refer to the concept of an emotion bank account. Actively listening generates a positive emotion bank balance. This helps you develop the flexibility in a relationship needed to deal with adversity and stress. You update your 'love map', as it were. Love maps refer to the space a partner occupies in the mind of the other half, to wanting to know what they are experiencing (Gottman, 1995).

Compassionate communication

Marshall Rosenberg's book *Nonviolent Communication* (2015) ties in well with the vision of the book you are currently holding. It serves as an important source of inspiration for this work. *Nonviolent Communication* provides readers with the tools needed to begin recognizing their own needs and to communicate them clearly, but also to listen to other people's stories with compassion, to their underlying needs and feelings. Applying the principles set out in *Nonviolent Communication* contributes to keeping relationships positive, and to the growth and development of yourself and others.

Nonviolent communication is an example from the field of humanist psychology as discussed in the introduction to this book. In the context of this book, we prefer the term 'compassionate communication', which we find to be more appealing. Compassionate communication is communication based on empathy and respect for others, but also based on respect and compassion for yourself. As such it ties in with the previous chapters, and contributes strongly to self-determination. Compassionate communication is based on Rosenberg's vision and methods. It can be applied to all possible relationships, including, for example, your relationship with your children, with pupils, with colleagues, with friends. As with all the skills covered in this book, compassionate communication requires practise and effort. If you find that the ideas of compassionate communication appeal to you, we can heartily recommend Marshall Rosenberg's *Nonviolent Communication* to help you broaden your insight into this type of communication, and to inspire you further.

Compassionate communication aims to build open and respectful relationships in which you clearly voice your needs and requirements. Part of this is also taking into account the needs of others. This is done by consistently applying the following four principles (Marshall, 2015):

1. Observing without judging

Your communication focuses on actual, concrete behaviours. Easier said than done, because in practice our observations are clouded in opinions – either subtly or explicitly. Examples of opinionated responses are:

- You are too passive;
- My father does nothing but complain; and
- Charley suddenly became very aggressive yesterday.

'Passive', 'complain', and 'aggressive' are all words that carry an opinion. Observations that do not include opinions or judgments would be:

- During the past few meetings, I have noticed that you have not said anything;
- Whenever I visit my father, he talks about how he feels our society is rapidly deteriorating;
- Charley shoved me as I walked past him.

If our opinion becomes part of the observation that we communicate to others, then chances are other parties will take our remarks as criticism. This often leads to a defensive attitude. Communications become less open, and others will not be as willing to listen to what you actually have to say.

2. Recognizing and expressing feelings

The second step to compassionate communication is expressing your feelings. Feelings are often confused by thoughts, evaluations, or interpretations of the behaviour of others.

This may lead us to say:

- I feel I am rubbish as a football player;
- I do not feel as if I am taken seriously; and
- I feel pressurized.

Whereas expressing your feelings should actually look like:

- I feel disappointed in myself as a football player;
- I feel frustrated; and
- I feel upset.

Another pitfall is overgeneralizing. We might say: 'I do not feel right.' That may be because we do not exactly know or dare to express our actual feelings. Phrased more specifically, we might say: 'I feel despondent' or 'I feel sad'. By expressing our feelings, we make ourselves seem vulnerable; it humanizes us. This is also a form of open communication, which improves the chances that other parties will be understanding of what we have to say. Others will be more willing to listen and comply as a result.

3. Relating feelings to needs

We often hold the cause of our feelings to be due to the behaviour of others, or due to circumstances. We are implicitly accusatory to others.
    This is expressed in our saying:

- You disappointed me when you did not show up; and
- It really ticks me off when you say that.

Relating your feelings to your needs, however, would lead you to say:

- I was disappointed in the fact that you did not come by this morning, because there was something I wanted to talk to you about, and wanted your opinion on; and
- It ticks me off when you say that, because I want you to respect me, and now I feel as though you are not taking me seriously.

Relating your feelings to your needs means you assume responsibility for your own feelings. This leads to a more efficient form of communicating, because it helps others imagine themselves in your situation, leading them to respond compassionately. It also avoids having others comply with your wishes based on guilt – which is a real contributor to disrupting relationships in the long run.

We frequently fail to express our needs openly and directly. This actually means we are not being respectful to ourselves. Or maybe we do express our needs, but use some sort of justification for them. We might say: 'Would you do the groceries and cook dinner? I have been cooking all week and I just feel exhausted right now. I feel I have earned a little me-time.' This often leads to negative responses, because others may view our justification as some sort of attack or demand. Expressing your need would be better phrased as: 'I need to take a long walk for some quiet introspection. Would you do the groceries and cook dinner today?'

Marshall Rosenberg uses a dark comic story involving his mother to explain what can happen if people are not open about their feelings. When his mother was 12 years old, her sister had to be admitted to hospital for a few days. To relieve her misery, her sister was given a lovely beaded pouch. Rosenberg's mother, in an effort to get such a lovely pouch for herself, faked a serious pain in her side. When her doctors were unable to find anything wrong with her, they decided to perform keyhole surgery in hospital. And lo and behold, Rosenberg's mother was given a lovely beaded pouch of her own. Then, when an orderly placed a thermometer into her mouth, she showed off her prize – but the orderly mistakenly thought she was offering her the pouch as a present, and accepted it graciously. Rosenberg's mother did not dare tell the orderly that this was not what she had had in mind. All her efforts had been for nothing.

4. Requesting what you need to enrich your life

The final step in compassionate communication is by using active language, and concretizing what we need from others. Our requests are often framed in vague and abstract language.

We might say:

- I need you to put more effort into our relationship; and
- I need you to respect my privacy.

If we are to be more specific, we should say:

- I would like us to agree to spend Wednesday evenings and Sundays together without you working or scheduling appointments of your own; and
- I would like you to ask for permission before entering my room.

By phrasing our requests more clearly, we increase the chances of others meeting our actual needs. Crucially, a request should be just that; not a demand in disguise. If others do not meet your request, and you become upset, then your request was actually a demand. Demanding something in this way means that you do not respect others' needs. Our thoughts often automatically transform requests into demands. Examples of these thoughts are: 'I will be the one to say what is acceptable', 'I am in charge', 'He should be doing what I asked', 'I deserve more money', 'Handing out punishment is well within my rights.'

We develop positive relationships when we know and express our feelings, when we recognize and voice our needs, when we make sincere requests instead of setting implicit demands, or try to have things our way through applying force or generating guilt. Chances are excellent that compassionate communication fuels mutual empathy and understanding. The first step is to be aware of your feelings and needs; because if these are not clear to you, communicating them to others is impossible.

Insufficiently recognizing your feelings and needs and failing to express these feelings and needs comes at a high cost. It leads to communications and behaviours inspiring alienation, conflict, and distancing. We become accusatory to others, we label people, we gossip, we distance ourselves, or we manipulate others into getting what we want.

If someone does something we do not like, one of the most frequently found responses is to classify their behaviour as negative, and to analyse it as such. A partner who wants more affection is demanding or dependent, while your need for affection is of course the result of a distant and insensitive partner. Colleagues who put in a lot of overtime are showing off or pushing themselves, but if you put in a little extra time, your colleagues are lazy slackers. Classifying others like this means we are actually raising the importance of our needs over those of others, forcing our own values on needs on them. The result is negative relationships and responses based on fear, guilt, or shame. These responses then lead to an eventual decrease in self-worth, to holding grudges or passive aggressive behaviour, not voicing your anger but displaying it indirectly.

Compassionately listening to others

The four elements of non-violent communication can also be applied to compassionate listening to the needs of others. This is a form of active listening which, despite what someone is saying, you are able to tell what they perceive, feel, need, and ask for. You can apply this, for example, if someone is behaving accusatorily or aggressively. You choose not to act defensively or to launch a counter-attack. You can summarize what you have heard in the form of questions. As a result, attacks, insults, and criticisms will generally begin to decrease, and the other's unfulfilled needs will come to the surface. Clearly this is not easy to do, and it is something that takes practise. Certainly, at first it may feel unnatural to respond in this was. But if listening sincerely and compassionately is your true intent, it is hard to go wrong.

Here is an example of a phone call between a father and a grown-up daughter, with the father striking an accusatory tone to his daughter whom he feels does not visit him often enough. He voices his displeasure almost immediately after she says hi.

Daughter: Hi, this is Anna.

Father: Oh, Anna. (Cold response.)

Daughter: Yes, it is me. How are you guys doing?

Father: It has been a while since we last saw you. When are you coming by?

Daughter: You sound disappointed that I have so little time to come see you.

Father: Yes, why can't you free up more time for your mother and me?

Daughter: I cannot free up any more time than I am doing. I understand from your response that you are missing me, is that right?

Father: Yes, that is right. I feel lonely. Your mother's health has taken a rapid turn for the worse, and I would really like to talk to you about that.

Daughter: I am sorry to hear about mom, and I am sorry to hear you are feeling lonely. Would you like to talk to me about it?

Father: Yes, I would like that.

Once the father's need and request have been established, the tone of the conversation changes. This is an example of compassionate listening which involves the daughter listening to her father's feelings, needs, and request, and giving feedback based on what she has heard. It is hard to listen compassionately if the other party directs criticism or anger at you. It is easy to become apologetic, or to turn critical in return. That is why questions, aimed at addressing feelings, needs, and requests, are such a powerful tool: They help you to avoid becoming defensive. The previous example would not have looked the way it did if Anna had immediately turned defensive.

Apart from turning defensive, compassionate listening and responding is made more difficult by other hurdles, such as: offering advice ('Maybe next time you could try . . .'), being pedantic ('Can't you look on this as something positive?'), offering comfort ('I am sure it will be fine . . .'), negatively reinforcing ('That must be so hard on you . . .'), questioning ('When exactly did this first happen?'), providing corrections ('It would have been better if you had . . .'). These are hurdles in that they remove your full focus on the other person.

Rosenberg describes how this form of listening is a form of rising above oneself: It is an opportunity to help those who are in pain.

Forgiveness

That which applies to life in general also applies to relationships: Relationships are a mixture of positive and negative events. At some point in our relationships, we are inevitably hurt to a greater or a lesser degree by the other person. Especially for those relationships in which you experience high levels of commitment should you give thought as to how to deal with that fact. There is so much in the relationship to experience that is positive, and there is so much love or friendship to be found, that you would much prefer the relationship to remain ongoing. This is where the ability to forgive comes in.

One frequently found response to being severely hurt by another's behaviour is experiencing feelings of vengefulness. Karremans and Van der Wal (2013) discuss how revenge is a natural response, which has some value in terms of survival. 'Punishing' the other person reduces the chances that the offending behaviour will occur in future. Expressing negative feelings or distancing yourself from the other person demonstrates, for example, that the other person hurt you. It helps you define a clear line which should not be crossed. But when negative feelings go unchecked, they may undermine your relationship. Positive relationships cannot exist if the parties involved are unable to forgive each other.

You will know you have truly forgiven the other person once your negative feelings, thoughts, and behaviours directed at them have strongly reduced or disappeared altogether. It is possible to forgive another person only to a certain degree. Karremans and Van der Wal discuss the overwhelming evidence that the ability to forgive is beneficial to relationships in both the long and the short term. Married couples who have a forgiving nature, for example, have been shown to be happier with their relationship than married couples who are not as forgiving. Couples who are forgiving are less prone to dredging up the past during an argument. Forgiving another person does not require you to still have a relationship with them. People you have not seen in a while, even those who have passed on, may be forgiven. Forgiveness does not require the other person to be around.

The ability to forgive also has tremendously positive effects on the forgiving person's physical and mental health. People who are capable of forgiveness suffer fewer physical complaints, worry less, and experience less stress and better sleep. Forgiving is made easier if the other person shows genuine remorse. People with high levels of self-appreciation or greater empathic skills (who are generally more able to put themselves into another person's position) are better able to forgive others.

In addition to forgiving someone else, it is possible that you were the one who hurt someone else, and that *that* person is forgiving *you*. In that case, you are also required to take up an active role: Being forgiven does not mean that this forgiveness is comprehended or recognized. This comprehension and recognition requires you to be compassionate towards yourself, to your clumsiness or your flat-out mistakes. If another person has forgiven you and you keep holding on to your feelings of guilt and shame, then that is simply needless torture. We all make mistakes.

Developing positive relationships – exercises

Exercise 1: Active and constructive response to good news

For the coming week, pay attention to how you respond to good news told by other people around you. Have another look at the different ways of responding on page 126. Try to be active and constructive in your responses. This does not mean you should take someone to dinner every time they tell you a positive titbit, but you should at least express your compassionate joy and keep actively asking questions. Focus your attention on the person telling the story. This is one way of contributing to a positive relationship.

This will also make it clearer to you how other people respond to your positive news. Do they respond actively and constructively? Who does, and who does not? If someone does not respond the way you would like them to, you can communicate that to them compassionately; see Exercise 4.

Tip

In some situations, you might very well experience jealousy when someone else tells you their story. This does not need to be a hindrance to responding actively and constructively. You can establish and recognize your jealousy, and even voice your feelings: 'I must admit to some jealousy; I would not mind if that happened to me. But I am happy for you'.

Exercise 2: Active listening

Practise active listening every day, or at least very frequently. For example: Ask a colleague how they are doing, and do so with the intention of taking the time to listen to their response actively. Of course, you should not avoid applying active listening should the situation spontaneously present itself if someone asks for your listening ear, or wants to talk to you.

Active listening entails:

- Picking the right moment. If you have an appointment in two minutes, then that is a bad time for an active listening session. If you are focused on something else, then that is also a bad time for an active listening session. It is a sign of diligence that you can indicate this fact and, for example, agree to get back to someone later.

- Choosing the right location. Someplace where you will not be easily distracted or interrupted. For example: Go for a drink somewhere quiet, and take a walk together.
- Focusing and engaging. Make the other person the centre of attention and truly connect with them. Make eye contact, make your posture look accessible.
- Giving the other person room. Allow them the space they need to tell their story: keep your encouraging responses and gestures to a minimum, allow the other person to finish speaking, do not try to fill any silences, do not respond with your own experiences or opinions.
- Reflecting. Tell the other person what you experience and hear; feed the essence of their story back to them. This lets you check whether you have correctly understood the other person, and lets them know you have understood them.

Active listening also means avoiding certain things:

- Judging/moralizing. This is true of both criticism and praise alike. Voicing your opinion means you have not truly been listening to the other person, and will force the other person's story into a different direction. Negative responses make people close off. But praise can also trigger people into not telling you what they actually wanted to share.
- Denying/Downplaying. Diverting attention, (logical) reasoning, comforting: These are also responses which make others close off.
- Providing solutions. Advising, asking excessive and inappropriate questions. An overly swift or inappropriate response will trigger a speaker to stop speaking freely.

Ian McWhinney (cited in Robertson, 2005) had the following to say about active listening:

> You can learn to be a better listener, but learning it is not like learning a skill that is added to what we know. It is a peeling away of things that interfere with

listening, our preoccupations, our fear, of how we might respond to what we hear.

Learning to listen actively and reduce your inhibiting responses can take time. Try not to judge yourself if you cannot do it immediately. Notice and recognize whatever is interfering with your active listening, and then refocus on the other person. Notice and recognize the fact if you should find yourself offering solutions, belittling experiences, or judging, and voice this recognition to the other person. Tell them you are sorry, and that you will try to avoid doing that. If you only notice you have been doing it when the conversation is over, resolve not to do it again.

As part of the exercise, review your day every evening. Were there moments where you did or did not listen actively? Replay some of your conversations in your mind's eye. What went well, what are you proud of? What can you resolve to do better next time? Be aware that you can also return to some conversations the next day, reflecting on the information or meaning of what another person told you.

Exercise 3: Express gratitude

One specific form of active response is actively expressing gratitude. There are several ways you can apply this concept:

- Voice your gratitude to the person concerned;
- Send a message or card expressing your gratitude; or
- Write an extensive letter and read it to the person you are grateful to.

The latter form may seem excessive. But in some situations, it can have real, added value as an experience shared by you and another. For example, imagine someone that you have known for a long time, and who truly means a lot to you. Explain to them what they mean to you in your letter, and actually read it to them. This may seem daunting, but personally delivering your message will make it come alive.

You will be able to see their response, and react to it yourself if applicable.

Exercise expressing your gratitude these coming weeks.

Tip

Remember:

- Only express gratitude you genuinely feel. Being grateful is not a trick; and
- Do not exaggerate: Be appropriate.

The following exercises are about compassionate communication.

Exercise 4: Your greatest current needs

Positive living is founded in recognizing and expressing your needs and hearing and recognizing those of others. Knowing your underlying needs precisely is not always easy. See below a list of some needs. Most of these are more or less present in all of us. Some needs can be stronger during certain periods. Review the list and answer the following questions:

Overview of needs

- *Self-care, joy and relaxation:* for example, safeness, protection, shelter, fun, enjoyment, exercising, health, recovery ...
- *Autonomy and individuality:* for example, self-expression, creativity, privacy, independence, free expression of opinions, authenticity, autonomy, relaxation ...
- *Connectedness and relationships:* for example, love, physical closeness, touch, respect, appreciation, gratitude, friendliness, sharing experiences, inspiration, honesty, attention, compassion, acknowledgement, social safeness ...

- *Connectedness and spirituality:* for example, faith, contemplation, reading, meditation, meaning, passion, silence, stillness, harmony, being in nature . . .
- *Competence and activity:* for example, learning new knowledge and skills, developing strengths, play, stimulation, challenges . . .

Questions about needs

1. Which of these needs that you experience (strongly) are currently being met?
2. Which of these needs that you experience (strongly) are currently not being met?
3. Which of these needs do you wish were met more fully?
4. How could you help these needs be met more fully?
5. Which needs required the help of others?

Exercise 5: Communicate based on the four steps of compassionate communication

Have another good look at the four steps of compassionate communication, the examples and pitfalls (pages 129 through 132). If you feel like it, practise these for the coming weeks. Apply compassionate communication if one of your current needs is not being met and you need another's help, for example (see your answer[s] to question 5 under Exercise 4). Try to articulate your feelings and needs as clearly as possibly, and to be as concrete in your request as you can: How can the other person help to enrich your life? You should always keep in mind that the other person may decline your request – after all, a request is not a demand.

Try to listen to the other person's response compassionately:

- What do they perceive?
- What feelings do they express?

- What needs do they express?
- What do they request?

Try to notice and recognize any tendency to non-compassionate communication on your part, such as accusing or manipulating. Take a deep breath or have a time out if you do. If the conversation is not going the way you want it to, and the end result is a conflict, review what was said and done at a later time. Where did things go wrong? Is it possible you stopped listening compassionately? Did you become judgemental or accusatory instead of observing what was there and what was concrete? Was your request actually a demand?

If you cannot reach common ground with the other person, see whether you can fulfil your need in some other way. Compassionate communication can also be applied if another person's behaviour is bothering you. The first step is very important in this case: Articulate the other person's behaviour without any value judgement.

Compassionate communication takes time and effort to learn. You can find a list of works which contain various examples and exercises at the back of this book.

Exercise 6: Compassionate listening

During a conversation, try to apply the following elements of compassionate listening. This is a specific implementation of active listening:

- What does the other person perceive?
- What feelings does the other person express?
- What needs does the other person express?
- What does the other person request?

Respond based on what you hear in relation to these elements. Though it may be difficult at first, you can also apply this exercise if someone is criticizing, accusing, or aggressively accosting you.

You should realize the following:

- Compassionate listening clarifies matters: Feelings, needs, and requests come to the foreground clearly.
- Compassionate listening de-escalates matters: It is respectful and disarming. It provides you with the handholds you need to listen to the underlying message without responding to accusations or aggression defensively or with hostility.
- Compassionate listening improves relationships: Needs, wishes, and expectations are clarified, and the potential for another to be able to meet these becomes evident.

Exercise 7: Wish someone the best

This exercise is a continuation of Exercise 2 from Chapter 5.

- Have a seat, get comfortable, and relax. Realize that you are a human being with vulnerabilities and strengths, and that set-backs are part of life. Let this fact sink in. This is part of being human.
- Think of someone you care about: a child, a parent, a partner. Realize that they, too, are occasionally confronted with adversity and, just like you, need relaxation, happiness, health, and other good things.
- Ask yourself what they need right now. What could this person want for? Allow whatever word that best describes what you feel they need to come to the surface. Think of relaxation, rest, kindness, security, happiness, health.
- Now wish for this need to be fulfilled. Without knowing whether or not your wish is actually going to come true, say it in your head. Imagine the other person in your mind's eye, and say to yourself: 'I wish you happiness, I wish you happiness, I wish you happiness.' Some people find it helps to do this in time with their breathing, but this is not required.

Exercise 8: Expand your kindness to others

Every day, you encounter other people: Some you know very well, some you have never seen before. For example: You may find yourself paying for something at a till every week without having any idea of who the person operating it really is. The idea behind this exercise is to apply your kindness to everyday life. We are asking you to consciously wish good things to those people you hardly know. Keep it light, though, and do not overdo it.

Standing in line to pay for your groceries, for example, focus your thoughts on the people in front or behind you, or the lady operating the register, and wish them something kind: 'I wish you happiness', or 'I wish you good health'. There is nothing you need to change about your posture, all you have to do is voice your wish internally. If you are at a school playground, wish good things to the parents picking up their children: 'I hope you have a quiet night'.

This may feel awkward for you at first but, as with many things, once it becomes a habit it may help you to be less judgemental toward others. This will have a positive effect on your own well-being, because complaining about and judging others puts you into a negative mood.

Exercise 9: Forgive

Do you have a relationship or a friendship you would like to remain ongoing, but which is subject to negative feelings towards the other person based on one or more events?

Recognize to yourself what the consequences of these negative feelings are. Are they undermining your relationship in any way? Would you like to reduce the amount of negative feelings you experience? If so, the answers to the questions that are part of the following steps can help you to forgive the other person.

- The first thing to ask yourself is whether you have clearly articulated and voiced your feelings. Does the other person know how you feel? If not, then that could be the first step.

- Has the other person expressed their remorse? If they have not, and you need them to do so, you can use the four steps of compassionate communication (see page 129) to ask them to do so.
- Can you image yourself in the other person's position in any way? We do not mean to excuse their behaviour, but it is a way of allowing yourself the room to forgive them. Try to envisage yourself in the other person's situation, having gone through what they have gone through. Are there any circumstances that may have played a part in this situation?
- Can you remember any event where you hurt someone else, similarly to how you have been hurt? Did the other person forgive you for that? What did their forgiveness mean to you?
- What would your forgiveness mean to the other person?

Tip

Forgiving does not mean forgetting. Forgiving also does not mean you have to restore or intensify a relationship.

References

Aron, A., and Aron, E. (1986). *Love and the expansion of self: Understanding attraction and satisfaction.* New York: Hemisphere.

Aron, A., Norman, C.C., Aron, E.N., McKenna, C., and Heyman, R.E. (2000). Couples' shared participation in novel and arousing activities and experienced relationship quality. *Journal of Personality and Social Psychology, 78,* 273–284.

Driver, J.L., and Gottman, J.M. (2004). Daily marital interactions and positive affect during marital conflict among newlywed couples. *Family Process, 43,* 301–314.

Fincham, F.D. and Beach, S.R.H. (2010). Of memes and marriage: Toward a positive relationship science. *Journal of Family Theory and Review, 2*, 4–24.

Gable, S.L., Reis, H.T., Impett, E.A., and Asher, E.R. (2004). What do you do when things go right? The intrapersonal and interpersonal benefits of sharing positive events. *Journal of Personality and Social Psychology, 87*, 228–245.

Huston, T.L., Caughlin, J.P., Houts, R.M., Smith, S.E., and George, L.E. (2001). The connubial crucible: Newlywed years as a predictor of marital delight, distress, and divorce. *Journal of Personality and Social Psychology, 80*: 237–252.

Karremans, J.C., and Wal, van der, R.C. (2013). Vergeving (Forgiveness). In: E.T. Bohlmeijer, L. Bolier, G.J. Westerhof, and J.A. Walburg (eds). *Handboek Positieve psychologie: Theorie, onderzoek en toepassingen. (Handbook Positive Psychology: Theory, research and applications).* Amsterdam: Boom uitgevers Amsterdam.

Reis, H.T., and Gable, S.L. (2003). Toward a positive psychology of relationships. In: C.L.M. Keyes and J. Haidt (eds). *Flourishing: Positive psychology and the life well-lived.* Washington DC: APA.

Reis, H.T., Smith, S.M., Carmichael, C.L., Caprariello, P.A., Tsai, F.F., Rodrigues, A., and Maniaci, M.R. (2010). Are you happy for me? How sharing positive events with others provides personal and interpersonal benefits. *Journal of Personality and Social Psychology, 99*, 311–329.

Robertson, K. (2005). Active listening: More than just paying attention. *Australian Family Physician, 34*, 1053–1055.

Rosenberg, M.B. (2015, 3rd edition). *Nonviolent communication: A language of life.* Encinitas CA: Puddledancer Press.

Chapter 8

Beyond the self

Introduction

You could say that our lives comprise of four dimensions (Leijssen, 2007). The first dimension is the physical. Important needs at this level are health, safety, external beauty, comfort, and pleasure. Taking good care of ourselves at this level involves healthy eating, enough rest and relaxation, and sufficient physical exercise. Transiency can be seen as an important threat to this dimension. As we become older, we irrevocably become subject to physical decay. Limited attention to this dimension is made in this book. There is a lot of information about healthy eating or exercise available elsewhere, for example, online.

The second dimension is the psychological. Important needs at this level are personal development, self-appreciation, competence, and self-determination. We aim for meaningful goals, we are creative, and we use and develop our strengths. The freedom to choose and the responsibility which characterize our existence can be seen as threatening. This dimension has been covered extensively in Chapters 2 through 6.

The third dimension is the social. Attention, care, cooperation and play, connectedness, and appreciation by others are important needs at this level. These needs can be realized through positive, quality relationships. To be able to do so, it is important to invest in our relationships, and that the needs of both parties are met. Open and honest communication is key. Loneliness, ostracism, guilt, and shame can be seen as major threats. This dimension has been covered extensively in Chapter 7.

The fourth dimension is the spiritual. Self-transcending ideals, meaning, and connectedness to a greater whole are important needs at this level. These needs are realized through selfless acts (altruism), support to others, meditation, religion, religious conviction, or experiencing the sacred in everyday life. Senselessness, violence, fear (of death), and the finiteness of things (in death) can be experienced as threats within this dimension. This chapter covers the spiritual dimension.

Before looking at the subject of spirituality, we would like to note two general considerations about the four dimensions. The first is that, generally speaking, you can say that you need to strike balance between these four dimensions in order to be able to lead a satisfying life. We are of the opinion that it is next to impossible to cope without one or more of these dimensions in our lives. Attention to your body safeguards your temper, and ensures you rest and recover sufficiently. Attention to the psychological safeguards your uniqueness, your individuality. It ensures that you remain loyal to yourself and your core values. Attention to the social safeguards interpersonal dialogue, outside perspectives, support, and love. It ensures that you retain a connection to other people. Attention to the spiritual safeguards inspiration and your appreciation of the greater good, caring for this and future generations. As a society, it ensures that we uphold certain norms and values without having to enforce them by law.

The second consideration is that you can go overboard in any of these dimensions. Going overboard can be the result of experiencing the threats within a particular dimension too strongly. The physical dimension may see a preoccupation with pleasure (by way of addiction, for example), with physical appearance, with the material. This preoccupation takes away room from the other dimensions. Preoccupations in the psychological dimension may involve egocentrism, self-interest, or self-importance. This reduces room for others, for silence, for reflection, for enjoyment. The social dimension may see a preoccupation with appreciation and recognition from others; the risk is becoming fully dependent on others, taking away any room for self-determination or individuality. The spiritual dimension may be subject to preoccupations focusing on fanaticism, elitist behaviour, or proselytizing; this risk is losing the connection to your body, to others, to reality. It is all about balance and finding the middle ground, both within and between the different dimensions of our existence.

We will address spirituality in the next paragraph. The type of spirituality discussed here does not necessarily involve religion – it can be experienced as a factor of your daily life as well.

Connectedness and spirituality

Previous chapters have focused mainly on the individual, aiming at personal growth and individual development. It is impossible, however, to only be focused on yourself – you are part of a greater whole, and everything you do or do not do has an impact on other people and the world around you. Our individualist society tends to let us see ourselves as separate from others, making ourselves the centre of our attention. Others are met with fear and mistrust. Occasionally, we do realize we are part of a larger group, for example, as a member of a family, of a group of colleagues, of a sports team – but even then, we tend to keep a small, accessible view. We see the group to which we belong as an extension of ourselves, and other groups as competitors or threats. The formation of a group is still a form of separation: us versus them. This makes sense from an evolutionary standpoint because the survival chances of the individual are greater if it is part of a group that sees other groups as potential threats.

Notably, many people who practise conscious living discover many corresponding values, such as love and compassion, in addition to discovering that they wish to be of meaning to others in society – beyond the self and beyond the groups they are a part of. A spontaneous need to widen their perspective comes into being, no longer focused on the 'I' but on a greater whole, leading us to realize that we are fundamentally connected to each other, to nature, to the world. This requires us to open up to others and to the world around us: It is also known as transcendence.

Transcendence means realizing that both the 'self' and the 'greater whole' exist simultaneously. These are not experienced as being separate, but as being closely connected. Transcendence does not mean letting go of your personality or 'self', because to function as part of the world the 'self' is essential. You are an individual, with you own wishes, needs, disapprovals, emotions, behaviours, qualities, and learning experiences. And in the meantime, you are also part of a great whole, able to transcend your 'self'. Once people become aware of the connection between the whole and the 'self', and begin to develop self-transcending values, we call this 'spiritual growth'. Spiritual growth can be stimulated by certain religious movements, but may also be separate from these.

Psychologist Tara Brach (2004) differentiates between vertical and horizontal spirituality. Practising vertical spirituality involves the practitioner attempting to connect to a 'higher' power or to arrive at a peak experience, like an enlightening spiritual experience or an experience which dissolves the 'self'. These experiences are special, but also unusual. Horizontal spirituality, on the other hand, involves the practitioner attempting to connect to the current moment, and therein find inspiration and connectedness. All religions and spiritual movements have examples of vertical and horizontal spiritual practices. In this chapter, we will focus on horizontal spirituality.

British psychologist William Bloom (2011) describes spirituality as the creation of a connection to the awe-inspiring power of nature, the cosmos, and existence, living according to self-transcending values and subservience. He describes three basic activities shared by all religions and spiritual traditions, namely: connecting, reflecting, and serving. He calls these the core skills required for spiritual development. If you are familiar with certain religious traditions, you will recognize these core skills. However, you do not need to feel or become connected to any tradition in order to apply these skills in your life. They are suitable for anyone who wishes to widen their perspective away from the 'self' and to look for inspiration in the mundane.

Connecting

People in a process of spiritual development experience how their consciousness expands and connects to a greater power or dimension. This power can be described in many ways, and you may have your own name for it. Examples are: the mysterious, God, inspiration, the well of life, nature, the source, the light. These are all terms for the same thing, and people who connect to this dimension describe the experience as loving, compassionate, inspirational, and wise. Nowhere in literature do we encounter anyone experiencing this power as aggressive or negative. This is notable.

There are different ways of connecting to the higher dimensions, to transcend ourselves. The exercises in this chapter cover several possibilities. Note that self-transcendence is only ever possible by retaining a connection to yourself. We do not feel the idea is to dissolve into a greater whole, but instead to experience yourself as a living being as part of the whole. One way of doing so is by being in touch with your body. Many movements also know this as 'earthing' or 'grounding', or having an 'inspired body' (see Exercise 1, page 160). The idea is to be present within your physical form.

And how does one experience the connection to that power or dimension outside oneself, full of kindness and wisdom? The answer to that question is found in your daily life; all you have to do to experience it, is to open up to it. You may have experienced it already. We asked people around us to explain when they feel connected to the dimension we described. Here are some of their statements:

'I was sitting on a bench in Paris. It was very busy, and I saw people bustling all around me. I just sat there quietly for a minute, feeling my body and the sun on my skin. I felt a calmness come over me, and realized I was sitting there with all those people with their own lives and troubles. I had a feeling of community. It was a peaceful sensation.'

'I have been running marathons for years, and I can feel my body respond once I hit a certain distance. This is a feeling also known as "runners high". I become fully absorbed in running, as though I am dissolving and on my feet at the same time. I feel at one with the moment.'

'When I am gardening and I look at the plants slowly raising their heads following the trials of winter, it makes me realize the wonder that is nature. It is a feeling of interplay: my hands and the remarkable force of nature.'

'Every yoga class I go to ends with a relaxation exercise: "Feel your own body, feel its boundaries, and let yourself flow outward like an oil stain". I always notice my physical boundaries fading away, and feel myself become as one with my surroundings. I am struck by this experience every time: I feel myself expand as I lose sight of all of my daily worries.'

'A walk through the countryside is enough to make me realize the miracle of everything. I am part of that miracle. Creative ideas just come to me as I am walking; I experience nature as a source of inspiration.'

'When my mother passed away. I was devastated, of course, but at the same time there was something else, something I cannot describe, something that just was.'

'Looking at my dog, lying on the grass all quiet. One paw tucked partly under him. How is it possible that something like him came to be? It takes my breath away.'

'When I am meditating, quietly sitting on my meditation seat. I am aware of my mind, the noises around me, my feelings, the space I am surrounded by.'

'At a concert, is that even possible? When I am among the dancing crowds I become fully absorbed in it, and feel the music thrum through my body. Inspiration finds its way to the audience through music. I become one with everything around me; for a moment, I feel a stillness within me and think of nothing at all.'

How is this for you? When do you feel touched, as though there is more than just yourself and your small inner circle? When do you feel inspired or as though you are being recharged? For some, it can be in quiet, natural surroundings; for others, at a crowded bar or during a rock concert. We recommend that you put this question to your friends or colleagues. The statements above tell us that there are many ways of connecting to the 'something' outside ourselves, and there is not one single best way of doing so. The same experience is felt during vastly different circumstances: The 'smaller self' becomes transparent, we experience expansion and wonder, our daily worries become part of the background. In order to connect, all you need to do is create those circumstances that will make it easiest for you to experience the connection, and to seek out and experience it as often as you can. Bloom describes how these experiences can be reinforced by paying attention to *what* is happening *while* it is happening. The concertgoer can become aware of the unification, the stillness; the gardener can become aware of the interplay between hands and nature.

Now ask yourself when you do not feel this sense of connection at all. These are often times when you feel completely absorbed by yourself and your daily worries, when you feel fear, or when you have closed yourself off in your own (little) world. Many people are constantly in this state of separation from the whole, and they only need a small opening to break through. The art is in finding that opening.

Reflecting

Reflecting is the second core skill that Bloom considers to be essential to spiritual growth. Reflecting begins with the willingness to stop, take a moment, and ask yourself questions about the way in which you approach life. The importance of reflection can be found in various religious or spiritual movements. People have the ability to examine and to reflect on themselves; this is part of having a developed brain, as we discussed on page 86. If you are never aware of what you think or how you feel, you cannot possibly experience growth, or break through the ingrained patterns that inhibit growth and that may be harmful to yourself or others.

In recent years, a lot of attention has been paid to practising meditation or mindfulness, and if this is something that appeals to you, we would like to recommend the suggested reading list at the back of this book. Practicing meditation is aimed at exploring yourself, among other things, and is exceptionally well suited as an awareness tool. Through meditation, you learn to observe yourself and your responses from a distance. Awareness can be reached by many other ways as well, but whatever method you use, self-reflection is most effective if it comes from a compassionate and relaxed mind-set (see Chapter 5, page 88). If you look critically in your view of yourself, you will activate your danger system which will cause your perspective to narrow, making it harder for you to arrive at the insights you need to help you grow.

Reflection might be mistaken with self-analysis or obsessively sifting through your life looking for explanations and solutions. The need for explanations and solutions is born from a need for control; but the more you think you know for certain, the more you will have limited yourself. In that case, reflecting will soon turn to worrying. You will begin to relapse into what is familiar and ruminate on the available information, but there is more and different information and intelligence available for those of us who open our minds. Chapter 6 described the difference between worrying and reflecting (see page 106); new perspectives are not born from worry. Reflection that is born from a place of stillness, from your connection, interest, and curiosity, is a reflection that is born of an open mind – which in turn opens up a world of possibility. A well-known Zen Buddhist saying is that of 'Beginner's mind, open mind', which advises the reader to keep an open mind as would a beginner. The open mind needed for proper reflection can be developed by applying the following five aspects to your life:

1. Regularly consider and welcome whatever is happening, do not suppress anything, do not turn away from whatever is calling your attention;
2. Be present by grounding yourself in the moment;
3. Focus on what is happening now, do not wait for what is coming, and do not pine for what is passed;
4. Allow yourself to relax and to find peace in current circumstances; and
5. Allow yourself to be ignorant.

Reading a book such as this one and taking part in the exercises actually also means you are reflecting. A wonderful form of reflection is to take a few minutes at the end of the day and just review. It allows you to stop and consider whether you have met your own needs and intentions.

Kindness and giving (serving)

This book is about helping yourself grow and blossom. We have looked at this from several perspectives: developing life enjoyment, utilizing your strengths, being optimistic, growing through adversity, developing flow, applying self-compassion and self-appreciation, and maintaining positive relationships. These are things you can enjoy and be content with, but it does not have to stop there; even more so, it should not stop there. Selfishness is a pitfall. What is the use of developing yourself and then not making your qualities available to the world; not caring or being compassionate for anyone beside yourself and your inner circle; not feeling involved, instead closing your eyes to the suffering of animals, human beings, or the world's problems in general?

Earlier, we wrote about how people who become more aware spontaneously develop the need to be meaningful to others and to society. Bloom (2011) describes several self-transcendent core values that appeal to people who are developing themselves spiritually. These core values are: charity, righteousness, compassion, protecting and caring for nature, giving love, respect, and affection, and radiating kindness. These values entail a certain promise, namely that you intend to act on them should you need to. Spirituality expresses itself in everyday life through applying self-transcendent values as actions, and being somewhat dispassionate about this.

In this context, dispassionate means acting according to your values, but doing so calmly. You do what is within your power, you realize and accept that the results of your actions cannot always be controlled, and you ground yourself in the moment ('what is, is'). People who only focus on achieving certain outcomes tend to become exhausted and bitter. The desired outcome may be self-transcendent (peace, animal welfare, elderly care, nature conservation, compassionate care), but the drive may be born from your need to assert yourself or to prove you are right. Emotions like fear and anger may be cloaked by the benevolence of the action, whereas an action born from transcendent values is associated with faith in life itself.

The following story about Ingrid, an elderly care worker in a nursing home, is a good example of dispassionate, self-transcendent action. Ingrid stands up for her values without becoming pedantic, and risking her own position.

Ingrid works as a caregiver in a nursing home, and she feels offended by the way a certain group of the elderly are being treated. The old-timers concerned are people who are no longer able to stand up for themselves. There are too few staff available, and the decision has been made to change their incontinence pads only once a day, saving a lot of time. Ingrid feels this action is degrading, and discusses her feelings with management – who advise her to keep quiet about this issue unless she would prefer to look for employment elsewhere. Ingrid voices her displeasure at this, and that she understands the need to cut costs, but not if this involves a policy that is in direct opposition to what the stands for. She indicates that she intends to inform the patients' next of kin. Those family members eventually manage to turn the policy around. But from that moment on, Ingrid is accused of being disloyal to the organization; both her colleagues and management are ignoring her. Ingrid tells others that she still feels good about what she did, because she acted in accordance with her values – even though she got the short end of the stick.

Studies in positive psychology have shown that people who live in accordance with self-transcendent values experience a greater general sense of well-being. Martin Seligman (2011, p. 20) even indicates that performing a kind act is the strongest contributor to feelings of well-being compared to other exercises from positive psychology.

A specific form of kindness is giving something of yourself. One way of applying this principle is by performing a kind act for someone else once a week. Think of volunteer work, joining someone (you know to be lonely) for a cup of coffee, or offering some help. Lyubomirsky, Sheldon, and Schkade (2005) for example, found that having their test subjects perform a kind act for another person five times a week over the course of six weeks led these subjects to experience an increase in well-being compared to the control group. Similarly, Otake et al. (2006) found that an increased awareness of kindness and maintaining a kind disposition contributed to increased pleasant emotions. Layous et al. (2012) conducted an interesting investigation among 415 children aged nine to eleven. Half of these children were tasked with performing three kind acts per week over the course of four weeks. These acts could range from carrying somebody's shopping to sharing their lunch. The other half of the children were tasked with visiting three different locations, such as their grandmother's house or a shopping mall. At the end of the four-week period, the children who had performed the kind acts were significantly better accepted by their peers than the children asked to visit three locations. But in both groups, the children experienced increased pleasant emotions and life satisfaction. In 2013, the results of a study were published which investigated the relationship between volunteer work and mortality rates (Okun et al., 2013). The researchers came to the conclusion that elderly people who worked as volunteers had an approximately 47 per cent greater chance of a longer life than those who did not work as volunteers.

Bloom describes how, in addition to our physical acts, we can also influence our surroundings by the feelings and intentions we radiate outwards, and that we can assume responsibility for this. You may have walked into a room which felt steeped in an unpleasant atmosphere. A team meeting can end with many of the internal frustrations remaining unresolved – and this frustration and anger can linger in the room following the meeting. Another example: You come and immediately sense that your partner is annoyed with something, even before a word has been said. Alternatively, you can also walk into a room and immediately sense that everything feels right. In the spring of 2013, we visited a cottage in England which felt suffused by a sense of soothing calm. We both experienced this exceptional feeling as we opened the door; we immediately felt at home, relaxed. The owner had taken great care in decorating the cottage, from a small vase of flowers to a kind, modest welcome email to us, her guests. When we left, and wrote something in the guestbook, we noticed that previous guests had also all experienced this sense of peace and calm. Many visitors, it turned out, felt this cottage was a place of quiet, which they kept returning to. It is clear that our environment influences us, and that we, in turn, influence our environment. It is good to be aware of this fact, and have the intention to take kindness with you wherever you go in day-to-day life.

Connecting – exercises

Introduction

The following exercises are about the spiritual experience of connection and about sources of inspiration. We recommend you first read this summary of the three characteristics of modern spirituality, as described by Bloom (2011, p. 18).

1. Connecting – The experience of being touched somewhere deep within, and of feeling connected to miraculous power of life;
2. Reflecting – Stillness, and quiet contemplation of the life you lead and the things you do, with the intention of learning, improving, and changing; and
3. Serving – Having a view of right and wrong, and acting in a way that is helpful to others.

Studying these three characteristics, you will probably realize that reflecting (2) and serving (3) are already partially described in the method to positive living as we have been describing it so far. Reflection is a concept that ties the book together; taking the time to contemplate your life, and how to improve its inspirational and positive basis. Earlier, we indicated that this is impossible without slowing down, without being more still as you give your undivided attention to everything you do, and approach yourself and others with kindness. The concept of serving is strongly rooted in compassionate communication, the basis for which is listening for the needs of others, and taking those into account as you try to help meet them as best as possible.

   The following exercises are mainly concerned with reinforcing your experience of connection. It is our conviction that experiencing and reinforcing connectedness helps you develop yourself and your positive way of living. First off are two grounding exercises. These are followed by an exercise intended to help you consider your needs concerning connectedness. Exercise 4 is more practical in nature. Exercises 5 and onwards are meant to help you experience and deepen your spiritual connectedness.

Exercise 1: Grounding exercise 1

There are numerous ways of relaxing your body and 'earthing'. Think of sports (hiking, cycling, running), yoga, tai chi, qi gong, body scans, or relaxation exercises. The following exercise is a short, powerful grounding exercise which will help you centre your body.

- Stand, with both feet at approximately the width of your hips. Make note of how your body feels, and whether you feel in touch with your body.
- Bend your knees as though you are about to jump. Take up a jumping position (knees bent, arms stretched backwards).
- Make a jumping motion without actually jumping. Your feet should remain on the ground.
- Experience the sensation in your body. You will probably feel the energy drain flowing downward, to your legs and feet.
- Enjoy the feeling of the experience as you end the exercise.

Exercise 2: Grounding exercise 2

Stand up straight, with both feet right next to each other. Your knees should be slightly bent, not locked into position. Keep track of several breaths; feel your breath flow into and out of your body.

Make note of how your body feels. Being in touch with your body means you will be able to feel the life energy it holds. You do not need to do anything special to feel this energy. Then, imagine how tall a tree stands, and imagine how you are standing as tall as a tree. Trees have strong roots that connect them to the earth. Their roots run deep, and provide them with nourishment and power. A tree is strong if its roots run deep. As a tree is rooted in the earth, so too are you rooted in life itself.

Feel your feet connect you to the earth. Every time you breathe in, imagine energy from the earth flowing into your body. Every time you breathe out, imagine your breath leaving you through your body and your feet into the earth. Breathe in, and feel the energy flow in. Breathe out, and feel your breath flow out. Breathe in and out like this for a minute.

Firmly rooted in the now, that is how a tree stands tall in its trunk. Stand tall in your body, and feel how firm you stand; this way, you will not be bowled over by any storms that blow through your life. Realize that taking good care of your body will help make you more resilient. Focus your attention on all parts of your body (your feet, legs, torso, arms, and head) for about a minute.

The crown, the branches, and the leaves of a tree are wide open and receptive. Fierce winds and storms may shake the branches, blow the leaves from the crown – but the tree remains rooted in the earth. Even though it may be shaken to the core of its trunk, a healthy tree holds its ground.

Life will continually feed you with new impressions, impressions to which you should be open and receptive. Realize that any storm in your life will pass. Realize that all things are transient. Remain anchored in the now.

Try to look at yourself and your surroundings with compassion. Take a compassionate look at your current situation in life, at the people around you, at yourself.

End the exercise by stretching and moving around.

Exercise 3: Clarify self-transcendent values and needs

Take the time to think about your values and your needs. Have a look at the overview of needs on page 140 for inspiration. What is truly important to you at this moment?

Do you have spiritual or self-transcendent values? If you do, then consider whether you are acting in accordance with these values. If so, how does this make you feel? If no, what is stopping you? How does it feel not to live in accordance with these values?

Exercise 4: Observe your kindness

Pay close attention to your own kindness for the next few days. How kind are you? How often do you take the time for someone? Did you ask questions? How thoughtful are you? What are the effects of being more or less kind? A mild way of performing this exercise is by reviewing your day. You can bask in the afterglow (see Chapter 1, page 19) of the moments in which you were kind, enjoying the effects on others and on yourself. If you notice that your kindness left something to be desired, make a mental note and resolve to do better tomorrow – or fix any outstanding imperfections.

Exercise 5: Be or give selflessly

An exercise aimed at sharing your positive life with others, is by doing something selfless for someone else this week. Give away some of your time by visiting someone, or take the time to ask someone if they need your help. That person might be a colleague, a neighbour, a family member. First, ask the other person whether they would appreciate your help. Having done this once or twice, once you feel that it gives you satisfaction and fits in with your values, you might consider making it a regular occurrence. You may already be working as a volunteer; you may already be helping others on a regular basis. In that case, we would like to invite you to consider the effects of your actions.

Exercise 6: Remember your moments of connection and inspiration[1]

Find a quiet moment and a comfortable place to sit. Try to recall a moment in your life when you felt touched by life's wonder and beauty, when your heart opened, or when you felt inspired. When was this? Try to recall the circumstances. What did you feel? What did you think? Was the experience powerful? Did it influence your life? The experience need not have been extreme; it may have been an everyday occurrence which helped you feel connected.

You may want to write your experience down; other memories and new experiences may join it over the coming days.

Exercise 7: Deepen your experience

Feeling connected to life's wonder, or feeling inspired, can happen at any time and under any circumstances. Think of a simple touch, of architecture, movement, of crisis and suffering, of dancing, sharing, animals, death, food, prayer, birth, running, helping, hobbies, comedy, cooking, art, landscapes and nature, meditation, music, education, parenthood, pilgrimages, poetry, loved ones, writing, sex, sports, studying, martial arts, walking, or singing.

Have another look at the moments of inspiration you wrote down under Exercise 5. Which circumstances present themselves? Write them down below. The list of circumstances may prompt new memories; add those circumstances to the list.

Under which circumstances and during which situations do you find it easy to experience a spiritual connection, and which of these could you easily and regularly incorporate into your life at fixed moments? You could look for an opportunity to improve your chances of experiencing connectedness, or to deepen your connection. Draft a concrete plan of action.

Exercise 8: Experience connectedness in daily life

There is a second exercise which can help you deepen and reinforce your experience of connectedness. Experiencing connectedness is made possible using four core skills (Bloom, 2011):

- The ability to be still and attentive;
- The ability to relax and ground yourself in your body;
- The ability to be kind in noticing what is happening; and
- The ability to surrender to the feeling of connectedness.

For the coming period, go over every day at the start of your morning. What is today going to bring? Usually, it will be a combination of recurring activities, such as cooking, shopping, and eating, combined with more specific activities, such as going to the cinema or meeting a friend. Pick an activity that appeals to you. Apply the aforementioned core skills to that activity; be still and attentive, relax in your body, notice what is happening, and surrender to the feeling of connectedness.

Note

1   These following exercises are based on exercises by William Bloom with kind permission (2011).

References

Bloom, W. (2011). *The power of modern spirituality: How to live a life of compassion and personal fulfilment.* London: Little Brown Book Group.

Brach, T. (2004). *Radical acceptance: Embracing your life with the heart of a Buddha.* New York: Bantam Books.

Layous, K., Nelson, S.K., Oberle, E., Schonert-Reichl, K.A., and Lyubomirsky, S. (2012). Kindness counts: prompting prosocial behavior in preadolescents boosts peer acceptance and well-being. *PloS ONE, 7,* e51380.

Leijssen, M. (2007). *Tijd voor de ziel. (Time for the soul).* Tiel: Lannoo.

Lyubomirsky, S., Sheldon, K.M. and Schkade, D. (2005). Pursuing happiness: The architecture of sustainable change. *Review of General Psychology, 9,* 111–131.

Okun, M.A., Wan-Heung Yeung, E., and Brown, S. (2013). Volunteering by older adults and risk of mortality: A meta-analysis. *Psychology and Aging, 28,* 564–577.

Otake, K., Shimai, S., Tanaka-Matsumi, J., Otsui, K., and Fredrickson B.L. (2006). Happy people become happier through kindness: A counting kindnesses intervention. *Journal of Happiness Studies, 7,* 361–375.

Seligman, M. (2011). *Flourish: A new understanding of happiness and well-being – and how to achieve them.* London: Nicholas Brealey Publishing.

Conclusion: a positive life as the art of living

Flourish

You have come to the end of this book. We hope you will take away something from what we have discussed, and that you will experience a positive change to the quality of your life.

We have based the information and ideas in the work on the concept of positive psychology. Positive psychology aims at helping people blossom. Within the field of positive psychology, this is more commonly known as 'flourishing'. Flourishing means finding the joy in your daily life, being able to develop yourself through meaningful activities and relationships, and feeling part of and connected to a greater whole. This may be part of society, or part of life as a whole. When you flourish, you will feel that you can contribute to these things.

The idea of flourishing was seen by humanist psychologists, such as Abraham Maslow or Carl Rogers, to be the essence of therapy. Maslow and Rogers refer to it as self-realization and authenticity. Each of us is unique, and each of us has their own unique potential. The art is in realizing your potential. This means being honest with yourself and others, recognizing your feelings and preferences, and communicating and acting based on them. You could call it 'living from the heart' or 'the art of living'.

Psychology and philosophy have experienced a huge increase in interest in the art of living in recent years, but the idea goes as far back as the days of Greek and Roman philosophers, such as Socrates, Aristotle, Seneca, Plato, Heraclitus, and Epictetus. They too concerned themselves with the question of what constitutes an optimum life, and what is our life's meaning. And they too spoke of the art of enjoyment, of self-reflection and self-exploration, of developing virtues and qualities, of developing values to serve as an inner compass, of transcending self-centeredness. The world may have changed phenomenally over two thousand years, but our fundamental questions are still the same.

A positive attitude to life

We would like to emphasize that flourishing, or positive living as we have termed it, is more of an attitude to life or a way of life than it is an end result. The intention should be to grow as a person, to bring out the best in yourself and others, to learn from what you do and experience. That is not the same as striving or expecting to always be in the most chipper of moods. Our book aims to help you set your sights on that positive attitude, that way of life, and to guide you along the way. Positive living is an ongoing process. Unexpected things can happen; life may challenge you, sadden you, force you to choose. But when you think about it, you will probably realize that growth without pain is difficult.

Basically, we are all able to find our inner wisdom. We are capable of discerning between the right and the wrong things to do; whether we do something because it feels right to us (from intrinsic, growth-oriented motivation) or because of 'illegitimate' reasons (from extrinsic, control-oriented motivation). When we choose the latter, we may be quite capable of finding explanations to justify our actions, but that does not mean they match who we are, or does not mean they will help us flourish. Every time we choose a non-authentic option, we become so slightly guilty of denying the creative, original person we are. We do not experience the life joy and deep satisfaction that are part of flourishing. The risks with waiting too long to develop and grow are that it may suddenly feel too late, even though it never really is too late. A serious life event (a serious accident or illness, or a sudden awareness of the transience of life) can be a wake-up call. Suddenly, people discover what it is that truly matters to them. They find love, the unusual in the usual, the miracle of life. But then, why wait for your wake-up call?

Fear as an obstacle

Positive living is not always easy. One of the things that can make it hard is the fear we all carry with us. This can be the fear of loss, death, freedom, loneliness, failure, under-appreciation, hurt, pain, or exile. Positive living asks you not to live *out of* your fears, but to live *alongside* your fears. Living out of fear means continually comparing yourself to others. It leads you to crave security and control. It leads you to become dependent on or addicted to power (dominance), the material, appreciation, or recognition. It forces you to adjust, to think in terms of 'everyone for themselves': get your own affairs in order before looking around you. Living out of fear leads us to project our insecurities and unwanted characteristics onto others, and to assign labels to others.

Living *alongside* fear means being able to notice and permit fear. Positive living asks you to shoulder your fears and insecurities. It asks you to make choices that are not about control or safety, but about taking on new challenges that involve some level of uncertainty. Growth is always based on something new, and new means unknown. You can never know exactly where you will end up.

Love as an engine

One of the strongest bases for positive living is found in love. Think about it closely enough, and this realization becomes inevitable. Love offers us the possibility of transcending our fears and fear-inspired tendencies, and of transforming our fears into something else. Love is wanting the best for yourself and others. Love for others and love for yourself go hand in hand. Both love for others and love for ourselves urge us along the path to self-determination. Love makes us braver, more creative, more powerful, more authentic, more beautiful. Viktor Frankl describes how the love for his wife helped him survive the concentration camps. Love inspires joy and meaning in life, and leads to connectedness. Love is synonymous with attention and compassion. Attention and compassion allow us to recover from our hurts. Attention and compassion cannot express themselves in any other way than through the intention of making yourself and others grow by being aware of the needs of others and of yourself.

The potential for great love and fear are found in all of us. A life that is driven by love or a life that is driven by fear; these are available to all of us, whenever, wherever. But you make the call. You decide how to live your life.

Sources of inspiration

Positive living, as we have said, is not always easy. Life can sometimes be incredibly hard on you. It is a matter of ups and downs, of picking yourself up and trying again. This is why self-compassion is so essential. Self-compassion starts with allowing ourselves to make mistakes, time and again; with allowing ourselves to get tripped up because we forget the things that are fundamentally important to us. We notice that ourselves all the time; and then we try and remember the ideas in this book and use them to our advantage. It is easy to be thrown off track when it comes to positive living, however temporarily. The demands that our society imposes on us are vast, such as the enormous increases in labour productivity. Economic progress thrives on consumption patterns that match high standards of living. So much attention is paid to status, to the external. Our society is becoming more high intensity, more efficient – but it is also becoming increasingly less personal.

So, take heart in the fact that there are many sources of inspiration available. You should always make time to energize yourself; go for a walk through the countryside, read biographies of people who inspire you, read inspirational books, take up yoga classes, attend (online) lectures, read poetry, talk to like-minded people (either in person or online), join a mediation group, visit churches, and so on. Be inspired.

Reference

Rogers, C.R. (1961). *On becoming a person: A therapist's view of psychotherapy.* London: Constable.

Recommended further reading

On positivity and positive emotions

Fredrickson, B.L. (2009). *Positivity*. New York: Three Rivers Press.

On discovering and using strengths

Linley, A., Willars, J., and Biswas-Diener, R. (2010). *The strengths book: Be confident, be successful, and enjoy better relationships by realising the best of you.* Coventry: Capp Press.

On flow

Csíkszentmihályi, M. (2008). *Flow: The psychology of optimal experience.* New York: HarperCollins Publishers.

On optimism

Seligman, M. (1990). *Learned optimism: How to change your mind and your life.* New York: Knopf.

On compassion

Gilbert, P.G. (2009). *The compassionate mind*. London: Constable.

Gilbert, P.G., and Choden (2013). *Mindful compassion: Using the power of mindfulness and compassion to transform our lives*. London: Constable & Robinson Ltd.

Neff, K. (2011). *Self-compassion: Stop beating yourself up and leave insecurity behind*. New York: HarperCollins Publishers.

On coping with adversity, acceptance of difficult emotions and posttraumatic growth

Bohlmeijer, E.T. and Hulsbergen M.L. (2013). *A beginner's guide to mindfulness: Live in the moment*. London: McGraw-Hill.

Joseph, S. (2011). *What doesn't kill us: The new psychology of posttraumatic growth*. New York: Basic Books.

On positive relationships and communication

Rosenberg, M.B. (2015, 3rd edition). *Nonviolent communication: A language of life*. Encinitas CA: Puddledancer Press.

On modern spirituality

Bloom, W. (2011). *The power of modern spirituality: How to live a life of compassion and personal fulfilment*. London: Little Brown Book Group.

Index

Note: **bold** page numbers indicate tables; *italic* page numbers indicate figures.